Microsoft Office®

EXCEL 2003

Editions ENI

BP 32125
44021 NANTES Cedex 1

Tel: 02.51.80.15.15
Fax: 02.51.80.15.16

e-mail: publishing@ediENI.com
http://www.eni-publishing.com

Straight to the Point collection directed by Corinne HERVO

Foreword

The aim of this book is to let you find rapidly how to perform any task in **Microsoft Office Excel 2003**, which is part of the Office 2003 suite. Each procedure is described in detail and illustrated so that you can put it into action easily.

The final pages are given over to an **index** of the topics covered and an **appendix**, which gives details of shortcut keys.

The typographic conventions used in this book are as follows:

Type faces used for specific purposes:

bold   indicates the option to take in a menu or dialog box.

italic   is used for notes and comments.

Ctrl   represents a key from the keyboard; when two keys appear side by side, they should be pressed simultaneously.

Symbols indicating the content of a paragraph:

▷   an action to carry out (activating an option, clicking with the mouse...).

⇨   a general comment on the command in question.

⌀   a technique which involves the mouse.

A   a keyboard technique.

a technique which uses options from the menus.

Table
of Contents

CHARTS AND OBJECTS

LISTS OF DATA

GROUP WORK

VARIOUS ADVANCED FEATURES

APPENDIX

1.1 The Excel environment

A - Starting/leaving Microsoft Office Excel 2003

▷ Click the **start** button, point to the **All Programs** option, then **Microsoft Office**, then click **Microsoft Office Excel 2003**.

▷ To leave:

File	Click the ✖ button	Alt F4
Exit	in the application window	

You may be prompted to save changes you have made in the documents which are open (the **Yes To All** option saves all open documents).

⇨ *If a shortcut has been created on your Desktop, double-click the* **Microsoft Office Excel 2003** *icon to start the application.*

B - The workscreen

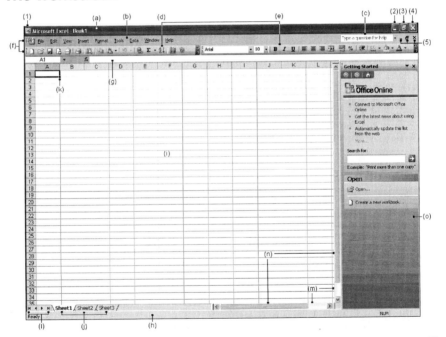

(a)   The title bar with the **Control menu** icon (1) and the **Minimize** (2), **Restore** (3) and **Close** (4) buttons. Below these, there are the workbook window buttons: **Minimize Window, Restore Window** and **Close Window** (5).

(b)   The menu bar; Excel menus are variable. When you open a menu, only the last options used appear. To see all the options, click the ⚇ symbol at the bottom of the menu or wait 5 seconds or make sure you open the menu with a double-click.

(c)	The **Type a question for help** box, in which you can type keywords to search for in the Excel help.
(d)/(e)	The **Standard** and **Formatting** toolbars.
(f)	The move handle, which you can drag to float a toolbar or menu bar.
(g)	The formula bar, which displays the active cell's contents and in which you can enter or edit data.
(h)	The status bar, showing you information about the current work status.
(i)	The workspace. A worksheet is made up of **cells**; the black square at the bottom right of the active cell is called the **fill handle** (k).
(j)	The worksheet tabs show the name of each sheet.
(l)	The tab scroll bar has buttons for navigating within the array of sheet tabs.
(m)	The scroll bars are for moving within the current worksheet; they contain scroll arrows and scroll boxes (n) that you can drag.
(o)	The **task pane** is an area containing options for carrying out certain tasks rapidly, such as creating new workbooks, researching information, inserting clip art etc. By default, the **Getting Started** task pane opens when you start the Excel application.

C - Finding help on Excel features

▷ If the task pane is not open, use **Help - Microsoft Excel Help** or press F1 : if the task pane is already open, click the ▼ button on the pane's title bar then click the **Help** option.

Searching with keywords

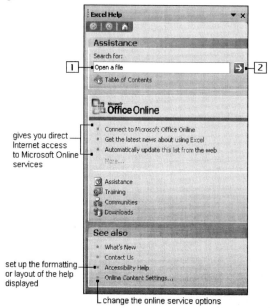

gives you direct Internet access to Microsoft Online services

set up the formatting or layout of the help displayed

change the online service options

1 Enter one or more keywords in this field.

2 Start the search.

*If your Internet connection is online, the search is carried out on the Microsoft Office Online web site and a message tells you that the search is under way; the number of help topics found and a list of those topics in the form of hyperlinks appear in the **Search Results** task pane. If you are working offline or if the keywords you enter do not correspond to those specified for the help file, the search result will be incomplete or you will obtain no results.*

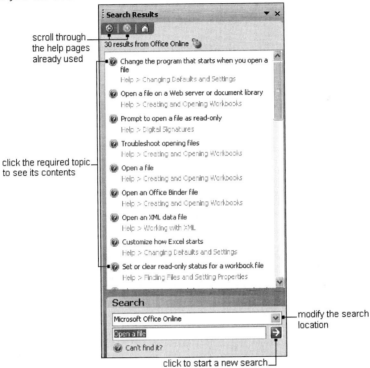

scroll through the help pages already used

click the required topic to see its contents

modify the search location

click to start a new search

⇨ *You can also make a keyword search using the* [Type a question for help ▼] *text box located on the right in the menu bar. Type your question or keyword right into the text box. Then, press the* [Enter] *key to start the search.*

Searching in the help Contents

▷ Open the **Excel Help** task pane. Then, click the **Table of Contents** link located in the **Assistance** frame.

If you are working online, Excel downloads information from the Microsoft Office Online website and displays the results:

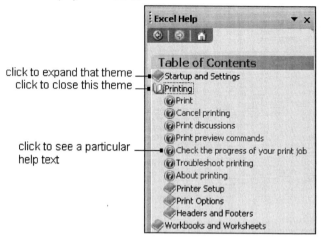

click to expand that theme
click to close this theme

click to see a particular
help text

If you are working offline, a message lets you know that more up-to-date information would be available online: working offline could limit the number of available help topics. If you are working online, the help topic's text appears in a separate **Microsoft Excel Help** *window.*

▷ When you are done with the help topic, click the ⊠ button to close the floating window.

⇨ *You can also use the* **Office Assistant (Help - Show the Office Assistant)** *for help, but you will have to install the Office Assistant component first.*

⇨ *To visit Microsoft's Office online services, use the* **Help - Microsoft Office Online** *command.*

D - Using the Research task pane

▷ Make sure your Internet connection is online.

▷ **Tools - Research** or 🖳

If a selected cell has data, this will automatically appear in the **Search for** *text box.*

▷ If you want to research something else, press Alt and click on the cell containing the text you want to research. You can also simply type in the text in the **Search for** text box.

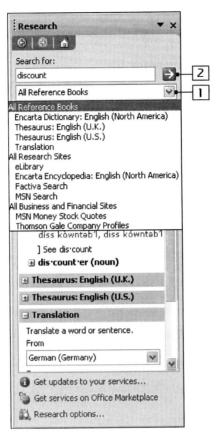

1 If necessary, open this list to choose the category or service in which you want to carry out your search.

2 Click to start the search.

The results you see depend on the search choice you made and the research options set.

▷ To expand the hierarchy of a category, click the ⊞ sign that is next to it; click the ⊟ sign to collapse the hierarchy.

⇨ *The first time that you use the **Translation** category, Excel may ask you if you would like to install the translation dictionary. Click **Yes** to begin installation. The installation will only take a minute and does not need a CD-ROM to work.*

⇨ *The **Research options** link in the **Research** task pane opens a dialog box for viewing the current research services and their properties and for choosing new services.*

1.2 Managing what appears in the window

A- Managing the task pane

▷ To display the task pane, use the **View - Task Pane** command or $\boxed{\text{Ctrl}}$ $\boxed{\text{F1}}$.

The task pane is anchored to the right of the application window.

▷ To change the contents of the task pane, click the ▼ button on the pane's title bar and choose the type of task pane you require.

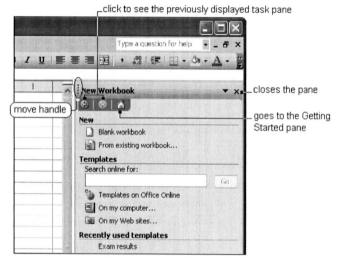

┌click to see the previously displayed task pane

closes the pane

goes to the Getting Started pane

move handle

Here, the task pane shows options for finding text.

▷ To move the task pane, point to its move handle (the pointer becomes a four-headed arrow), then drag the pane to the required position. Release the mouse button when the pane is correctly placed. To dock the task pane, drag it to one of the edges of the window; to make a floating task pane, drag it into the middle of the workspace.

▷ To close the task pane, use the **View - Task Pane** command again or click the ▣ button on the pane's title bar.

B- Freezing/unfreezing titles on the screen

▷ Click inside the column which follows the row titles you want to freeze, and/or click inside the row which comes after the column titles.

▷ **Window - Freeze Panes**

⇨ *To release the titles you have frozen, use **Window - Unfreeze Panes**.*

⇨ *You can also display two different parts of the worksheet simultaneously by splitting the window. To do this, drag the split bar located at the top of the vertical scroll bar*

▣ *and/or the split bar located at the right end of the horizontal scroll bar* ◄►| *depending on whether you want to split horizontally or vertically. This action produces two separate panes, each of which can display a different area of rows and/or* *columns, allowing you to work on two distant parts of the same worksheet. To remove the split, use the **Window - Remove Split** command.*

C- Zooming in on the workspace

▷ **View - Zoom**

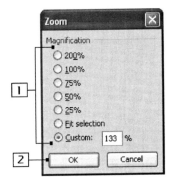

1 Choose the required zoom percentage, or type your own value into the **Custom** text box.

2 Click to confirm.

⇨ *The zoom scale can also be chosen from the* 100% *list on the **Standard** toolbar.*

⇨ *To fit the worksheet to the size of the screen, use the **View** - **Full Screen** command.*

D- Changing what is displayed in the window

▷ **Tools - Options - View** tab

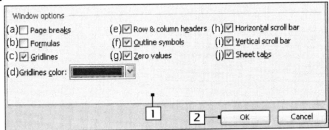

1 Choose to:

   (a)   display/hide page breaks (represented by a dotted line).

   (b)   display/hide calculation formulas instead of results.

   (c)   display/hide the spreadsheet's grid.

   (d)   change the colour of the gridlines.

   (e)   display/hide the letters and numbers at the top of columns/end of rows.

   (f)   display/hide the symbols accompanying an outline.

(g) display/hide all zero values; to hide zero values in selected cells, apply a custom format (namely 0;0;) to them.

(h) display/hide the horizontal scroll bar.

(i) display/hide the vertical scroll bar.

(j) display/hide the tabs of the sheets in the workbook.

2 Click to confirm.

E - Displaying/hiding an open workbook/a sheet

▷ To display a hidden workbook, use the **Window - Unhide** command; to hide a workbook, activate another workbook or use **Window - Hide** to hide the active workbook.

▷ To hide the active worksheet, use **Format - Sheet - Hide**; to display a sheet that is hidden, use **Format - Sheet - Unhide** and double-click the name of the sheet you want to see.

F - Managing toolbar display

▷ To use tools that are hidden on the **Standard** and **Formatting** toolbars when they are on one row, click one of the 🔘 buttons and click the tool button you want to use.

▷ To change the length of a toolbar when it shares a line with another bar, drag the toolbar's move handle horizontally.

▷ To display or hide a toolbar, right-click any toolbar:

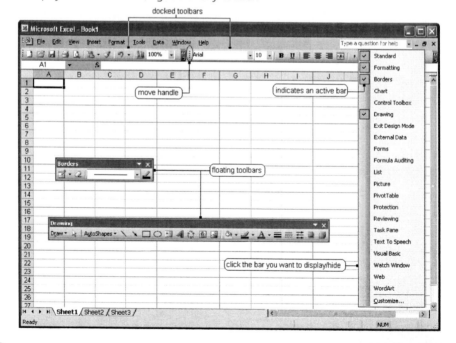

▷ To create a floating toolbar, drag the bar by its move handle into the middle of the workscreen. Release the mouse button when it is in the correct position.

▷ To dock a bar without choosing its destination, double-click its title bar.

⇨ When all the toolbars are hidden, you can find them using the **View - Toolbars** command.

1.3 Moving around/selecting in a worksheet

A-Moving around in a sheet

▷ Use the scroll bars:

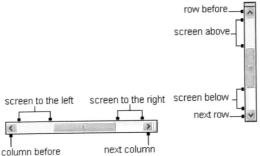

⇨ As you drag the scroll box, Excel displays the row number or the column letter in a ScreenTip.

A ▷ Use the keyboard:

cell to the right/to the left	→ or ⇄ / ← or ⇧ Shift ⇄
cell above/below	↑ or ⇧ Shift Enter / ↓ or Enter
screen to the right/to the left	Alt Pg Dn / Alt Pg Up
screen above/below	Pg Up / Pg Dn
column A in the active row	Home
cell A1	Ctrl Home

⇨ To reach a specific cell, select the active cell reference on the formula bar, type the reference of the cell where you want to go and press Enter .

B- Finding a cell

By its contents

▷ If you want to search the whole sheet, activate cell A1; otherwise select the range concerned.

▷ **Edit - Find** or Ctrl F

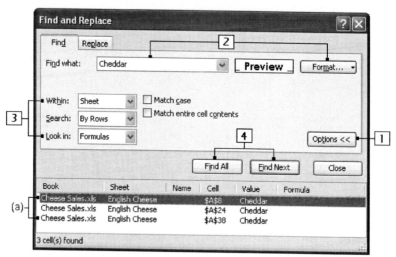

1. Click this button to display, and define, more search options.

2. Specify what you are looking for: to look for cell contents, enter them in the **Find what** box. To look for formatting, click the **Format** button and use the **Find Format** dialog box to choose the attributes you want to find.

3. Choose the search specifications.

4. To make the search cell by cell, click **Find Next**. Click **Close** if Excel finds the cell you were seeking; otherwise continue with **Find Next**.
   To look for all the relevant cells with a single action, click **Find All**. The list of found cells will appear at the bottom of the dialog box (a). Click one of the values in the list to select that cell and click **Close**.

⇨ The **Choose Format From Cell** option, which is in the list attached to the **Format** button, lets you select a cell in the worksheet to retrieve its formatting attributes for the search.

⇨ You can look for just a cell's contents without formatting, and vice versa.

⇨ Be careful, Excel remembers the last texts/formats you searched for; to cancel a text search, delete the contents of the **Find what** box; to cancel the formatting attributes, open the list on the **Format** button and choose **Clear Find Format**.

C - Moving from one sheet to another

▷ Using the tab scroll buttons, display the name of the sheet to which you want to go. Click the tab to activate the sheet.

first sheet
previous sheet
next sheet
last sheet
drag to change the space reserved for tabs

⇨ To scroll the tabs quickly, keep the ⬛Shift⬛ key pressed down while clicking ◀ or ▶.

⇨ On the keyboard you can use [Ctrl] [Pg Dn] to move to the next sheet or [Ctrl] [Pg Up] for the previous sheet.

D-Selecting cells

▷ You can select adjacent cells in three ways:

Dragging	Click the first cell of the selection and drag over the others. When you are satisfied with the selection, release the mouse button.
[⇧ Shift]-clicking	Click the first cell to be selected and then point to the last one. Hold down [⇧ Shift] then click at the same time. Release the mouse button before the [⇧ Shift] key.
On the keyboard	Hold down the [⇧ Shift] key and use the appropriate arrow keys.

▷ To select non-adjacent cells, select the first range of cells, hold down the [Ctrl] key and click or drag over the next cell or range. When you have finished, release the [Ctrl] key then the mouse button.

⇨ In a formula or dialog box, a selection of adjacent cells is symbolised by a colon (:), such as D4:D10 and a selection of non-adjacent cells is symbolised by a comma (,) such as C4,H1.

⇨ To select cells according to a specific sort of content, use the **Edit - Go To** command or [F5] or [Ctrl] **G**, click the **Special** button and double-click the type of cell that you want to select.

E- Selecting rows and columns

▷ The following methods can be used:

	Row	Column
🖱	Click the row number.	Click the column letter.
[A]	Activate a cell in the row and press [⇧ Shift] [space].	Activate a cell in the column and press [Ctrl] [space].

⇨ To select several rows (or columns) at a time, you can drag over them, or hold down [⇧ Shift] and click.

⇨ To select the entire worksheet, click the button in the top left corner, where the column containing row numbers meets the row containing column letters or press [Ctrl] [⇧ Shift] [space] or [Ctrl] **A**.

2.1 Managing workbooks

A- Opening a workbook

▷ **File**
  Open

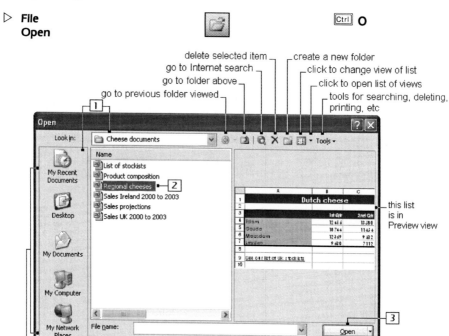

delete selected item
go to Internet search
go to folder above
go to previous folder viewed

create a new folder
click to change view of list
click to open list of views
tools for searching, deleting, printing, etc

this list is in Preview view

click to see other shortcuts
click a My Places Bar shortcut for quick access to a folder

[1] Open the drive and/or folder containing the document.

[2] Select the document (you can open several documents at once: use the Ctrl and/or ⬆Shift keys to select them first)

[3] Click to open the workbook (you can also simply double-click the file icon).

⇨ *The names of the last four workbooks used appear at the end of the **File** menu: click one of them to open the workbook.*

⇨ *To add a shortcut to the **My Places Bar**, open the **Look in** list and click the drive, folder or Internet location for the folder to which you want to add a shortcut then use **Tools - Add to "My Places"**.*

B- Saving a workbook

A new workbook

▷ **File**
  Save

Ctrl S

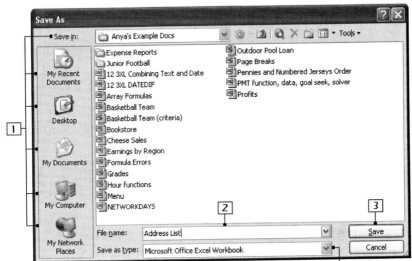

here, change the file type if you want to use
the Excel workbook in other application

1 | Activate the disk and the folder where the document is to be saved.

2 | Give the document's name (up to 255 characters, including spaces).

3 | Save the document.

⇒ *Excel documents have the extension .XLS (this may be hidden, according to the view options of your Windows Explorer).*

Existing workbooks

▷ **File**
  Save

  ‖Ctrl‖ **S**

⇒ *To save a workbook under a different name, use the **File - Save As** command or* ‖F12‖.

⇒ *To update the summary of a document, use **File - Properties** and fill in the **Summary** page.*

⇒ *To choose a default working folder, use **Tools - Options - General** tab and change the **Default file location**.*

C - Closing workbooks

▷ **File**   Click ‖X‖ in the   ‖Ctrl‖‖F4‖ or ‖Ctrl‖ **W**
  Close   workbook window

▷ Save the workbook, if appropriate.

⇒ *To close all open workbooks, hold down the ‖⇧ Shift‖ key as you open the **File** menu then click **Close All**.*

D-Creating a new workbook

▷ To create a workbook based on the standard template, click 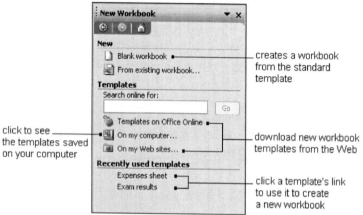 or press **Ctrl** **N**.
A new workbook, called **Book(number)**, appears on the screen.

▷ To create a workbook based on a template other than the standard template, use the **File - New** command to display the **New Workbook** task pane.

creates a workbook from the standard template

click to see the templates saved on your computer

download new workbook templates from the Web

click a template's link to use it to create a new workbook

▷ If you clicked the **On my computer** link, click the tab in the dialog box that corresponds to the folder in which the template is stored, then double-click the template's name.

▷ Enter your information into the new workbook then save it as any normal workbook (with **File - Save**).

⇨ To create a workbook from an existing workbook, click the **From existing workbook** link in the **New Workbook** task pane; select the workbook of your choice and click the **Create New** button. Excel opens a copy of your chosen workbook, temporarily giving it the same name followed by a number; save this workbook as if it were a new workbook.

E- Using e-mail

Sending a worksheet as the body of a mail message

This technique allows the recipient to read data produced with Excel, even if he/she does not have the application installed on his/her computer.

▷ Open the workbook then activate the sheet you want to send.

▷ **File - Send To - Mail Recipient** or

The first time you use this command, a dialog box appears and prompts you to specify if you want to **Send the entire workbook as an attachment** or **Send the current sheet as the message body**. You should choose the second option.

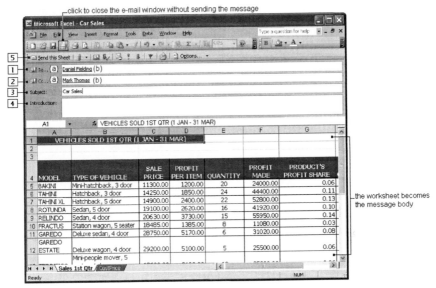

This screen may differ depending on the e-mail software used by default.

1. Indicate the e-mail address(es) of the recipient(s) by selecting them from an address book (a) or by typing them in (b) (use a semi-colon to separate each address from the next).

2. If necessary, indicate any addresses to which you want to send a carbon copy of the message, using an address book (a) or by entering them directly (b).

3. If necessary, change the message title.

4. If necessary, enter a comment.

5. Click to send a copy of the active worksheet to the mail recipient(s).

Sending a workbook as an attached file

Using this method requires the recipient to have Excel installed.

▷ Open or create the workbook you want to send.

You can send only a whole workbook and not a part of one.

▷ **File - Send to - Mail Recipient (as Attachment)**

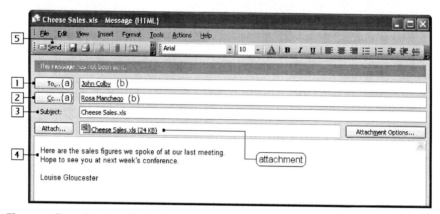

The e-mail application (Outlook 2003 in this example) opens a new mail message window.

[1] Select the addresses in the address book (a) or type them in (b), separating each address with a semi-colon.

[2] If you want to send any copies, select them from an address book (a) or enter the addresses (b).

[3] If necessary, change the title of the message.

[4] Click in this box then enter any comment or message you want to add.

[5] Click to send your message and attached file.

⇨ With Outlook 2003, each recipient receives a copy of the attached file by default. If you want a single copy of the attached file to be available to all the recipients in the document workspace of the SharePoint Services site of your choice, use the **Attachment Options** by clicking the button of the same name.

⇨ To open or change an attachment, the recipient must open the message and then double-click the attachment's icon. Opening this file will start the Excel application automatically.

⇨ To close the e-mail window without sending the message, click the ❎ button. If you made any changes to the message, Excel prompts you to save the document. If you click **Yes**, the document will be saved in the **Drafts** folder, or in the **Inbox** depending on your software. You can send it at a later time.

2.2 Managing worksheets

A - Selecting several sheets at once

The objective behind selecting several worksheets at once is to make actions common to all the sheets, such as copying, deleting, entering data, formatting etc. Sheets selected in this way make up a "workgroup".

▷ To select several adjacent worksheets, click the first sheet's tab, hold down the ⇧ Shift key and click the tab of the last sheet required.
To select several nonadjacent sheets, click the first sheet's tab, hold down the Ctrl key and click the tab of each other sheet you require.
To select all the sheets in the workbook, right-click one of the sheet tabs and choose the **Select All Sheets** option.

▷ To select a single sheet again, deactivating the workgroup, click the tab of a sheet that is not in the selected group or right-click the tab of one of the selected sheets and choose **Ungroup Sheets**.

B - Copying/moving a worksheet

▷ Open the workbook containing the sheet you want to move/copy and, if you are moving or copying to another workbook, open the destination file too.

▷ Activate the sheet you want to copy or move or select the sheets concerned.

▷ **Edit - Move or Copy Sheet**

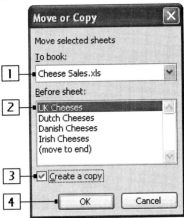

| 1 | Select the destination workbook.
| 2 | Select the existing sheet in front of which you want to insert.
| 3 | Activate this option if you are making a copy (deactivate it if you are moving the sheet).
| 4 | Click to transfer the sheet.

⇨ *To move one or more sheets in the active workbook, click the tab of the sheet you want to move or select several sheets, then drag the tab(s) to the new position.*

C- Inserting worksheets

▷ Select the sheet before which you want to insert a new sheet; to insert several sheets at once, select as many consecutive tabs as you want to insert new ones.

▷ **Insert - Worksheet**

D- Deleting worksheets

▷ Select the sheet(s) you want to delete then use **Edit - Delete Sheet**.

▷ Confirm your decision by clicking the **Delete** button.

E- Changing the colour of worksheet tabs

▷ Select the tab(s) concerned.

▷ Right-click the tab or one of the tabs if you have selected several and choose the **Tab Color** option.

▷ Select the colour of your choice and click **OK** to confirm.

When the sheet is active, its name appears underlined in the chosen tab colour.

⇨ *You can also use the* **Format - Sheet - Tab Color** *menu option to modify your selected tab(s).*

F- Naming a worksheet

▷ Double-click the tab of the sheet you are going to name then type the new name over the former one. Confirm with Enter .

This name must not contain more than 31 characters including spaces. It must not be between square brackets nor include the following characters: colons (:), slashes (/), backslashes (\ ), question marks (?) or asterisks (*).

Excel 2003

3.1 Entering data

A- Entering constants (text, values, dates, etc.)

▷ Activate the cell where you want the data to appear then type the data.

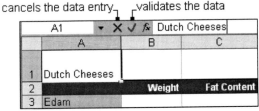

cancels the data entry — validates the data

▷ Activate the next cell you want to fill in.

⇨ *To enter several lines of data in a cell, press* Alt Enter *at the end of each line or use* **Format - Cells - Alignment** *tab and tick the* **Wrap text** *option.*

⇨ *To enter the same data in several cells, select all the cells concerned, type the data (a formula, perhaps) and press* Ctrl Enter *to enter.*

⇨ *Once you have typed in a few characters, Excel may suggest the rest of the entry based on the existing entries in the column (providing there is no more than one empty cell between the rest of the list and your entry). This is the AutoComplete feature, which is active by default, and which can be deactivated using the* **Enable AutoComplete for cell values** *option in the* **Options** *dialog box (***Tools - Options - Edit*** tab). If the suggested entry is suitable, enter; otherwise, to see the full list of potential entries, use* Alt ↓. *Click the entry you wish to use. If you do not want to use any of the AutoComplete suggestions, continue typing or press* Del *then* Enter *to confirm your initial characters.*

⇨ *The* **Move selection after Enter** *option available in* **Tools - Options - Edit** *tab activates or deactivates moving on to the next cell when you press the* Enter *key.*

⇨ *You can enter up to 32 767 characters in a cell.*

⇨ *If you type a number with your default currency symbol (e.g. £10000 or $10000), Excel will apply a currency format automatically (£10,000 or $10,000). To enter a percentage, type the % sign just after the number. To enter a negative value, precede the number with a minus (-) sign or place it in parentheses.*

⇨ *When you enter dates using only the last two figures, Excel interprets them like this: from 00 to 29 = 2000 to 2029 and from 30 to 99 = 1930 to 1999.*

⇨ *If you use Windows XP, you can change these default settings (numbers, dates, times, currency) using the Windows* **start** *menu -* **Control Panel - Regional and Language Options** *(or* **Date, Time, Language, and Regional Options***, depending on your view) -* **Customize** *button (or choose a task from the list).*

B - Inserting symbols

This technique inserts symbols that do not appear on your keyboard.

▷ Be in the cell where the symbol should appear, and type any preceding text if necessary.

▷ **Insert - Symbol - Symbols** tab

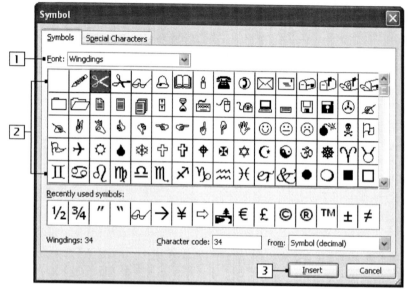

☐1 Select the font that contains the character you want to insert.

☐2 Select the required character.

☐3 Click to insert the character.

*The **Cancel** button becomes a **Close** button.*

▷ Close the dialog box with the **Close** button.

C - Inserting the control date into a cell

▷ Activate the cell where you want to display the date.

▷ There are three ways to insert the computer's control date:

=TODAY()	The control date, updated each time the sheet is opened.
=NOW()	The control date and time, updated when the sheet is opened.
Ctrl ;	The control date, not changed automatically.

▷ Enter.

D-Creating a series of data

▷ If the series' progression is to increment with an interval of a single unit, enter the first value in the series, and drag the fill handle of that cell up to the cell that will display the last value.
If the series' progression is to increment with an interval different to one, enter the values of the first two cells in the series. Select these cells and drag the fill handle of the second cell up to the cell that will display the last value.

	A	B	C	D	E	F
1		Product 1	Product 2	Product 3	Product 4	Product 5
2	Monday					
3	Wednesday					
4						
5		(fill handle)				

▷ Once you have created the series, an **Auto Fill Options** button appears in the bottom right corner of the series. By clicking this button, you can, if you wish and according to the nature of the series, choose to change the type of copy or the way incrementing occurs.

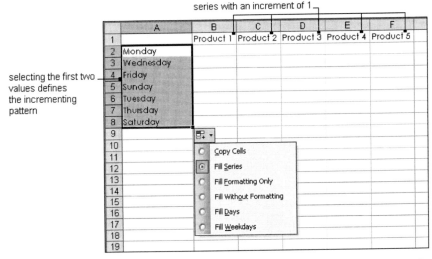

series with an increment of 1

selecting the first two values defines the incrementing pattern

⇨ You can also enter the first value of the series and select the cell containing that value, then use the **Edit - Fill - Series** command to define what type of series it is and how it should increment.

E- Creating a custom data series

▷ **Tools - Options** - **Custom Lists** tab

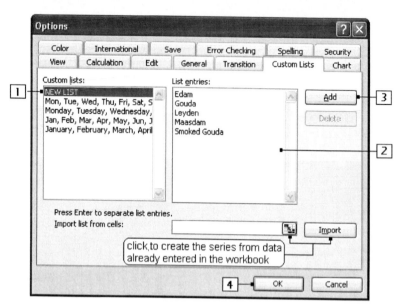

[1] Click **NEW LIST**.

[2] Enter the data, pressing [Enter] to separate each entry.

[3] Create the list.

[4] Click to confirm and close the dialog box.

⇨ *The first character of an entry cannot be a number.*

F - Attaching comments to cells

▷ Activate the cell where you want to make a comment then use the **Insert** - **Comment** menu option or [⇧ Shift] [F2].

▷ Enter the text in the comment box.

The comment is entered directly into a ScreenTip. Use [Enter] to change lines.

▷ Press [Esc] or click outside the box.

*A red triangle marks the top right corner of a cell that contains a comment. This indicator is visible only when the **Comment indicator only** option is active in the **Options** dialog box (**Tools - Options - View** tab).*

▷ To display a comment, point to the cell that contains the red triangle.

⇨ *To edit a comment, select the corresponding cell, then click* [icon] *on the **Reviewing** toolbar. To delete a comment, select the cell concerned, then click* [icon].

G-Defining authorized data

▷ Select the cells concerned.

▷ **Data - Validation - Settings** tab

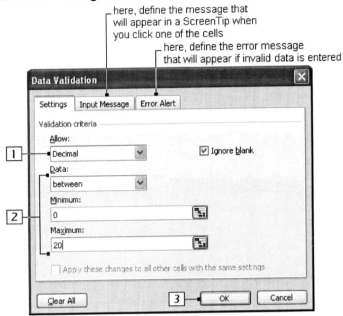

here, define the message that will appear in a ScreenTip when you click one of the cells

here, define the error message that will appear if invalid data is entered

[1] Specify the type of data authorized in the cell(s).

[2] Give your criteria, according to the type of data at hand.

[3] Click to confirm.

⇨ *Data already existing in the cells are not tested; you can however ask Excel to put red circles around cells containing values that do not conform to the validation criteria: do this with the ▦ tool button on the **Formula Auditing** toolbar.*

3.2 Editing data

A-Modifying cell contents

▷ Double-click the cell concerned.

▷ Make the changes (the ⌷Ins⌷ key switches between Insert mode and Overtype mode) then enter.

⇨ *You can also click the cell then edit its contents in the formula bar.*

B- Clearing cell contents

▷ Select the cells to be cleared.

▷ Drag the fill handle backwards over the selected cells to clear their contents, or press the ⌈Del⌉ key.

⇨ *This technique deletes the contents of the cells without affecting their format. The command **Edit** - **Clear** allows you to indicate exactly what should be cleared.*

C- Replacing cell contents and/or formats

Replacing text

▷ If the replacement is to be carried out over the active worksheet or all the worksheets in the workbook, activate a single cell. To make the replacement in a portion of the active sheet, select the range of cells concerned.

▷ **Edit - Replace** or ⌈Ctrl⌉ **H**

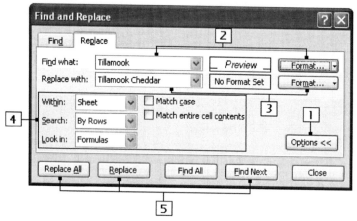

1 If necessary, click this button to see the replacement options.

2 In the **Find what** box, enter the text you are looking for and/or define the formatting you are seeking by clicking the **Format** button and activating the relevant options in the **Find Format** dialog box.

3 In the **Replace with** box, give the replacement text and/or define the replacement formatting by clicking the **Format** button and activating the relevant options in the **Find Format** dialog box.

4 Activate the appropriate search options.

5 Make the replacements one by one by clicking the **Find Next** and **Replace** buttons, or in a single action (**Replace All**).

⇨ *You can replace only text: check that the formatting preview reads **No Format Set** (otherwise, select the **Clear Find** (or **Replace**) **Format** option under the corresponding **Format** button).*

⇨ *You can replace only formatting; in this case, remove the contents of the **Find what** and **Replace with** text boxes.*

D-Sorting data in a table

▷ Select the table you want to sort.

▷ To sort by one criterion, activate a cell in the column you want to sort by. Then use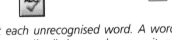
to sort in ascending order or ![A↓] to sort in descending order.

⇨ *To sort by several criteria, use the **Data** - **Sort** command.*

E- Checking the spelling in a text

▷ To check the whole worksheet, activate any cell. To check part of the text, select it.

▷ **Tools**   ![ABC✓]   [F7]
 Spelling

*Excel reads the text, stopping at each unrecognised word. A word may be unrecog-
nised, because it is absent from Excel's dictionary, because it contains an unusual
combination of lower case and capital letters, or because it is typed twice. Spelling is
checked against Excel's main dictionary, and against as many personal dictionaries as
you wish (by default, the only existing one is CUSTOM.DIC).*

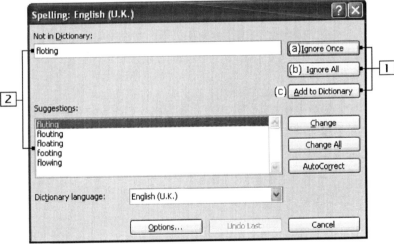

1. If the word is correctly spelt, click:

 (a)   to leave the word unchanged and continue the check.

 (b)   to leave a particular word unchanged each time it occurs in the text.

 (c)   to add the word to the current dictionary.

2. If the word contains a mistake, correct it by a double-click on one of the **Suggestions**
or enter the correct spelling in the **Not in Dictionary** box.
Next, click **Change** to replace the incorrect word with the correct one, or **Change All**
to replace the incorrect word with the correct one each time it occurs.

▷ For a word which is repeated by mistake, click **Delete** to remove the repeated word.

▷ At the end of the spelling check, click **OK** in the dialog box that appears.

3.3 Copying and moving data

A-Copying data into adjacent cells

▷ Activate the cell you want to copy then point to its fill handle.

March	Total
5,431.00	16,503.00
3,531.00	
3,546.00	

fill handle

▷ Drag the fill handle to the last destination cell for the copy then release the mouse button.

▷ Specify how you want to copy, by clicking the **Auto Fill Options** button at the bottom right of the copied range:

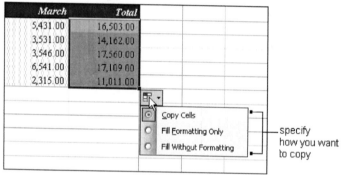

specify how you want to copy

B- Copying and moving cells

✍▷ Select the source cells.

▷ Point to the edge of the selected range (the pointer takes a ⟰ shape).

▷ If you are copying, press the [Ctrl] key and, without releasing it, drag the cells to their destination.

If the cells are being moved, just drag the cells to their new position.

▷ Release first the mouse button, then the [Ctrl] key, if you have been using it.

⇒ *To move a range of cells to another worksheet, hold down the [Alt] key as you drag the selected range onto the tab of the sheet concerned then to the first cell of the destination range. To copy cells to another worksheet, hold down both the [Ctrl] and [Alt] keys as you drag.*

▷ Select the source cells.

▷ If you are copying the cells, use:

Edit
Copy

[Ctrl] C

If you are moving the cells, use:

Edit   Ctrl **X**
Cut

▷ Activate the first cell of the destination range.

▷ To copy contents and formats, use:

Edit   Ctrl **V**
Paste

*When you paste copied data, a **Paste Options** button appears at the bottom right of the destination range so you can choose further copying options.*

▷ To choose what you want to copy, open the list attached to the [tool] tool button.

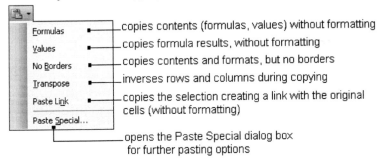

Formulas	copies contents (formulas, values) without formatting
Values	copies formula results, without formatting
No Borders	copies contents and formats, but no borders
Transpose	inverses rows and columns during copying
Paste Link	copies the selection creating a link with the original cells (without formatting)
Paste Special...	opens the Paste Special dialog box for further pasting options

⇨ *You will find these same options when you use the **Edit - Paste Special** command.*

C - Copying cells into several sheets

▷ Select the cells you want to copy.

▷ Select the other worksheets involved, by holding down Ctrl or ⇧ Shift and clicking their tabs.

▷ **Edit - Fill - Across Worksheets**

▷ As required, choose to copy **All** or just the **Formats** or just the **Content** and click **OK**.

D - Using the Office Clipboard

▷ If necessary, display the Clipboard task pane with **Edit - Office Clipboard** or, if the task pane is already on screen, click the ▼ button at the top of the pane and choose **Clipboard**.

▷ Select the cell(s) or object you want to cut/copy and transfer it to the Office Clipboard with the **Cut** or **Copy** command in the **Edit** menu.

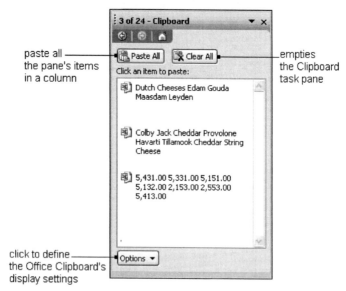

paste all
the pane's items
in a column

empties
the Clipboard
task pane

click to define
the Office Clipboard's
display settings

*The **Office Clipboard** contains all the items (a maximum of 24) cut or copied from the various Office applications (Excel, Word, PowerPoint etc.).*

▷ To paste one of the items from the **Clipboard** task pane, activate the first destination cell then click that item. Insert each item in this way, as many times as required.

*When you point to an item, an arrow appears on its right. Click this arrow to see options allowing you to **Paste** or **Delete** the item.*

▷ If necessary, close the **Clipboard** task pane by clicking its ⊠ button.

E - Reproducing a format

▷ Select the cells whose formats you want to copy then click ▨ on the **Standard** toolbar.

A paintbrush appears under the mouse pointer.

▷ Select the cells to which you want to apply the format.

⇨ *If the formatting has to be reproduced several times, double-click the ▨ tool button. Press ⎡Esc⎤ to cancel this function.*

⇨ *You can also copy formats by making a standard copy/paste operation then clicking the **Paste Options** button ▦ at the bottom of the copied cells and choosing the **Formatting only** option.*

F- Making simple calculations while you copy

▷ Select the data you wish to copy and use **Edit - Copy**.

▷ Activate the first destination cell (the target cells must contain some data).

▷ **Edit - Paste Special**

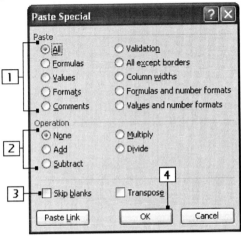

1 | Choose which elements you wish to copy.

2 | Specify the operation you wish to perform.

3 | If you want to omit any empty cells in the selection, tick this check box.

4 | Click to confirm.

G-Copying Excel data into another application and establishing a link

When a link is in place, any changes made to the data in the original Excel workbook are carried over into the file containing the exported data.

▷ Open the Excel workbook containing the data you want to copy and make your selection.

▷ **Edit** Ctrl C
  Copy

▷ Open the other application and the document into which you want to paste the Excel data.

▷ Put the insertion point where the data should be pasted.

▷ **Edit - Paste Special** (in the receiving application)

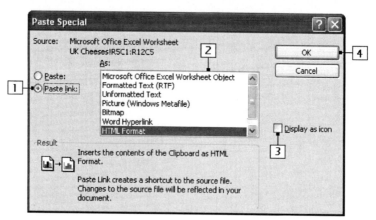

1 Activate this option.

2 Select the format in which you want to paste the data.

3 Activate this option if you want the linked data to be displayed in the form of an icon.

4 Click to confirm.

3.4 Named ranges

A-Naming cell ranges

First method

▷ Select the range of cells which you want to name then use the command **Insert - Name - Define** or Ctrl F3.

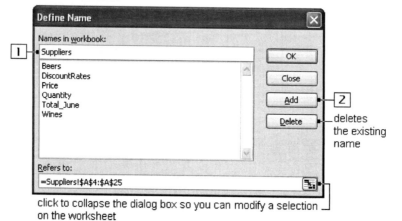

click to collapse the dialog box so you can modify a selection on the worksheet

1. Enter the name for the range (no spaces or hyphens).

2. Add the new name to the list.

▷ Go on to define any other names then click **OK**.

Second method

This method is useful if the names that you want to apply to the cells are adjacent to them.

▷ Select the cells containing the names to be used and the cells that you want to name.

▷ **Insert - Name - Create** or Ctrl ⇧ Shift F3

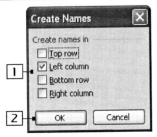

1. Indicate the position of the cells containing the names.

2. Click to confirm.

⇨ *To see the list of names and associated cell references in the worksheet, activate the first cell in which you want to display the list, use **Insert - Name - Paste** and click the **Paste List** button.*

B- Modifying named ranges

Changing which cells are associated with the name

▷ Select the new range of cells required then use **Insert - Name - Define** or Ctrl F3 .

▷ Enter the new name.

You must type in the name again and not simply select it from the list of names.

▷ Click the **Add** button and confirm with **OK**.

⇨ *You can also redefine the cells in a named range by selecting the range name in the **Define Name** dialog box, clicking the ▦ button and selecting the new cells in the worksheet.*

Changing the name of the range

▷ Insert - Name - Define or Ctrl F3

▷ In the list, select the name concerned.

▷ Enter the new name in the **Names in workbook** box then click the **Add** button and click **OK**.

This action does not delete the previous name.

C - Selecting a range of cells by its name

▷ Click the 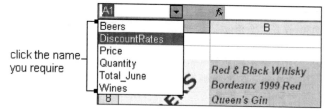 button on the left of the formula bar.

click the name
you require

4.1 Calculations

A- Entering a calculation formula

▷ Activate the cell which will display the result.

▷ Type =

▷ Activate the first cell involved in the calculation (click the cell or use the arrow keys to move the pointer).

▷ Indicate the mathematical operation to perform (+, -, /, *, % or ^ to raise to a power).

▷ Repeat for each of the cells involved in the calculation:

MEDIAN	▼ X ✓ ƒx	=(C3*D3)-E3			
A	B	C	D	E	F
2	Unit weight (kg)	Price per unit	Quantity	Discount	Total to pay
3 Edam	3.0	24.00	6	17.28	=(C3*D3)-E3
4 Gouda	3.5	25.00	5	15.00	
5 Maasdam	6.0	56.00	1	5.60	
6 Leyden	6.0	59.00	3	17.70	
7					

▷ When you reach the last cell, either click the ☑ button on the formula bar or press the ⎡Enter⎤ key.

⇒ *If you know the cell references you can type them in rather than using the mouse or arrow keys to point to them.*

B- Calculating with values from more than one sheet

You can enter a formula into one worksheet that refers to cells on a different worksheet.

▷ Activate the cell that is going to display the result.

▷ Type =

▷ Start the formula and at the appropriate place, click the tab of the required sheet, select the cell(s) you require, enter the required arithmetic operator and finish the formula.

▷ Press ⎡Enter⎤ or click ☑ to confirm.

B5	▼	ƒx	=Dutch!F3+Danish!F3+Belgian!F3		
	A	B	C	D	E
2					
3	European sales - all cheese types				
4		January	February	March	
5	Northern Europe	55441.51			
6	UK				
7	Ireland				
8					

In cell B5, we create a sum of the values in cells F3 on the "Dutch", "Danish" and "Belgian" worksheets.

CALCULATIONS

⇨ *You can also calculate values from several different workbooks. When doing this, make sure all the workbooks are open. Use the **Window** menu to go to a cell in a worksheet in a different workbook.*

C-Adding up a group of cells

▷ Activate the cell which is going to display the result.

▷ Click **Σ** or press ⌐Alt⌐ =.

MEDIAN	▼ X ✓ *fx*	=SUM(E6:E11)				
	B	C	D	E	F	G
4						
5		Quantity	Unit Price	Total		
6	Red & Black Whisky	9	14.50	130.50		
7	Bordeaux 1999 Red	2	3.20	6.40		
8	Queen's Gin	4	11.00	44.00		
9	Wild Chicken Bourbon	5	11.60	58.00		
10	Smirchoff Vodka	8	19.50	156.00		
11	White Vermouth	4	7.80	31.20		
12			Order total	=SUM(E6:E11)		
13				SUM(**number1**, [number2], ...)		
14						

▷ If you are not satisfied with this selection, change it by dragging.

⇨ *When you select a group of cells containing numbers, by default Excel displays the sum of these values on the status bar. If you right-click this result in the status bar, you can choose another function so you can display the average, the count of non-blank cells, the number of cells containing numbers (Count Nums), the highest (max) value and the smallest (min) value of the selection.*

D-Including an absolute cell reference in a formula

An absolute cell reference is a fixed reference that does not evolve when the formula is copied.

▷ Start entering the formula, stopping after the cell reference that you want to make absolute. If you are editing an existing formula, position the insertion point after the cell reference.

▷ Press ⌐F4⌐.

the $ signs show that the row and column references are absolute

MEDIAN	▼ X ✓ *fx*	=E7*F4				
	A	B	C	D	E	F	G
1	Salesperson	Miranda Boyle					
2	ID Number	12-560					
3							
4	Sales June				Commission	2.75%	
5							
6	File	Flights	Insurance	Other	Total	Commission	
7	04060103	560	25	0	585	=E7*F4	
8	04060305	1826	54	0	1880		
9	04060514	962	0	150	1112		

▷ Complete the formula if necessary, then enter.

⇨ *Press* F4 *again for only the row number to remain absolute, and again for the column number; these are known as mixed references.*

E- Using simple statistical functions

▷ Click the cell where the result will be displayed then open the list on the Σ ▾ tool button by clicking the black arrow.

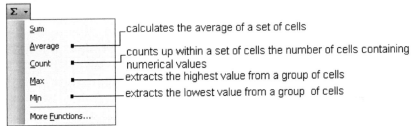

Sum

Average ● ─── calculates the average of a set of cells

Count ● ─── counts up within a set of cells the number of cells containing numerical values

Max ● ─── extracts the highest value from a group of cells

Min ● ─── extracts the lowest value from a group of cells

More Functions...

▷ If the suggested selection is incorrect, drag to modify it then enter.

F- Inserting a function

▷ Click the cell where the result will be displayed.

▷ Click the *fx* button on the formula bar or press ⇧ Shift F3 or use the **Insert - Function** command.

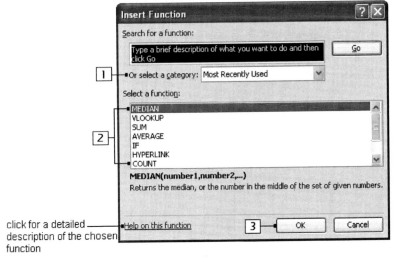

click for a detailed description of the chosen function

1 If necessary, change the category.

2 Choose your required function from the list.

| 3 | Click to confirm.

▷ To set each argument within the function:
- click the corresponding text box and click the  button,
- on the worksheet, select the cell(s) corresponding to the argument,
- click ▣ to restore the dialog box.

▷ When you have defined all the arguments, click **OK**.

⇨ *You can also insert a function within a formula or within another function. To do this, start the formula and at the appropriate place click the ▼ button on the formula bar. This displays a list of the last functions used and the More Functions option which takes you to a full list of functions.*

⇨ *To find a function easily, enter a brief description of the result you wish to obtain in the Search for a function text box on the Insert Function dialog box (Insert - Function) and click Go at the top of the dialog box. Excel will display a list of functions corresponding to your request.*

⇨ *If you know the formula you want to use, you can enter it directly into the cell. If you do this, a ScreenTip appears, showing the different arguments you must set.*

G-Using named ranges in calculations

Using a name in a formula

▷ Start entering the formula then stop where the name is required and use **Insert - Name - Paste** or ⬚F3⬚.

double-click the name of the range you want

▷ Complete the formula.

⇨ *You can also enter the name directly into the formula, instead of indicating the cell references.*

Replacing cell references with their names

▷ Select the cells containing the formulas you want to modify.

▷ **Insert - Name - Apply**

▷ Click all the names concerned. If you select a name by mistake, click it again to deselect it.

▷ Click **OK**.

If you select names that are inappropriate for that formula, Excel ignores those names.

H-Setting a condition in a formula

▷ Activate the cell where you want to display the result.

▷ Enter your condition, taking care to follow the syntax:
=IF(condition,action if TRUE,action if FALSE)

*You can insert the IF function and set each argument in the **Function Arguments** dialog box or enter the formula directly into the cell.*

C3	▼	f_x =IF(B3>=58,"Pass","")	
	A	B	C	D
1				
2	Student Name	Final Marks	Subject Result	
3	BAILEY Claire	69	Pass	
4	EVANS David	52		
5	JAKOVIC Elena	88	Pass	
6	MCPHERSON Anne	73	Pass	
7	NASH Elizabeth	54		
8	TAYLOR Duncan	68	Pass	
9				

If the student's mark in cell B3 equals or is higher than 58, the text "Pass" is displayed in the cell; if the mark is lower, no text is displayed.

⇨ *A variety of actions can be performed in a conditional expression:*

Display a number	enter the number,
Display a text	enter the text between quotation marks,
Display the result of a calculation	enter the calculation formula,
Display the contents of a cell	enter to the cell,
No display	type "".

⇨ *For conditions, several operators are available:*

>/<	greater than/less than
<>	different from
>=/<=	greater than or equal to/less than or equal to.

⇨ *You can set multiple conditions, linking them with the operators AND and/or OR: use one of the following functions, depending on your needs:*
if several conditions need to be met at the same time:
=IF(AND(cond1,cond2,....,condn),action to take if all the conditions are satisfied,action to take if any one condition is not satisfied)
if at least one of the conditions must be met:
=IF(OR(cond1,cond2,....,condn),action to take if at least one of the conditions is satisfied,action to take if none of the conditions are satisfied)
if several conditions are nested:
=IF(cond1,action to take if TRUE,IF(cond2,action to take if TRUE,IF(cond3,action to take if TRUE,action to take if FALSE)))

I- Calculating with dates and using date functions

▷ If you are calculating in days, proceed as for other calculations, since any date entered is treated as a number of days.

▷ If you want to combine text and a date from different cells, use the **TEXT** function with syntax **=TEXT(value,format_text)**. The **value** argument represents a numerical value, a formula with a numerical value result or a reference to a cell containing a numerical value: the **format_text** argument represents a number format in text form as defined in **Format - Cells - Number** tab - **Category** box.

	A	B	C	D	E
	A6		▾	ƒₓ ="Invoice date:"&TEXT(B2,"dd-mmm-yyyy")	
	A	B	C	D	E
1	Operation	Date			
2	Invoice date	5/6/04			
3	Date received	15/6/04			
4	Payment date	30/6/04			
5					
6	Invoice date:05-Jun-2004				
7					

▷ To calculate the difference between two dates, you can use the **DATEDIF** function, whose syntax is **DATEDIF(start_date,end_date,interval)**. The **interval** argument represents the unit of time used to calculate and can take on the following values: **"y"**, **"m"** or **"d"** to calculate a difference in years in months or in days, **"ym"** or **"yd"** to calculate the difference in months or days as if the 2 dates occurred in the same year or **"md"** to calculate the difference in days as if the 2 dates occurred in the same month.

	A	B	C	D	E
	A7		▾	ƒₓ =DATEDIF(B1,B2,"y")	
	A	B	C	D	E
1	Start date	01/02/1994			
2	End date	20/02/2004			
3					
4		Length in			
5	years	months	days		
6					
7	10	120	3671		
8					

—the interval argument here is "d"

└the interval argument in this cell is "m"

DATEDIF is one of Excel's hidden functions, so it does not appear in the **Insert Function** box or in the online help. These hidden functions were introduced into Excel for compatibility reasons.

▷ To add a number of months to a start date, use the following syntax:
=DATE(YEAR(start_date),MONTH(start_date)+period_in_months, DAY(start_date))

To add a number of years, use:
=DATE(YEAR(start_date)+period_in_years, MONTH(start_date),DAY(start_date))

For example to calculate the date two months from now, use:
=DATE(YEAR(NOW()),MONTH(NOW())+2,DAY(NOW()))

⇨ If the results of your calculations are four years ahead of what they ought to be, deactivate the **1904 date system** option in **Tools - Options - Calculation** tab.

J- Calculating with times and using time functions

▷ If you want Excel to recognize data as a time and save it as a decimal, you have to separate the various parts of the time with a colon (:). For example, you type 6.30 pm and 43 seconds as **18:30:43**. To avoid mentioning the seconds, type **18:30**.

Example of a time entry	Value recorded by Excel
00:00 (midnight)	0
11:59	0.499305555555556
12:00 (noon)	0.5
15:00 (3 o'clock)	0.625
18:00 (6 o'clock)	0.75

This way of defining time allows Excel to perform mathematical calculations on times. For example, to calculate the difference between 18:00 (6 pm) and 15:00 (3 pm), Excel calculates = **0.75 - 0.625 = 0.125** and the result is **03:00**.

▷ To calculate the difference between two times and show the result in standard time format, which is hours:minutes:seconds, you can use the **TEXT** function with this syntax **=TEXT(value,format_text)**.

The **value** argument represents a numerical value, a formula giving a numerical value result or a reference to a cell containing a numerical value.

The **format_text** argument represents a number format in text form as defined in **Format - Cells - Number** tab - **Category** box.

	A	B	C
1	Start time	08:30:45	
2	End time	15:15:00	
3			
4	Description	Result	Formula
5	number of hours between two times	6	=TEXT(B2-B1,"h")
6	number of hours and minutes between two times	6:44	=TEXT(B2-B1,"h:mm")
7	number of hours, minutes, and seconds between two times	6:44:15	=TEXT(B2-B1,"h:mm:ss")
8			

K- Using lookup functions

The lookup functions VLOOKUP (V for vertical) and HLOOKUP (H for horizontal) search for values in a table according to position. The lookup table is made up of a column (or row) that contains the comparison value (such as a product code): the other columns (or rows) contain values associated with the comparison value.

▷ Sort the table in ascending order on the data in the first column (or row).

▷ In the cell where you want to display certain information from the table, use the following function:
VLOOKUP (lookup_value,table_array,col_index_num,range_lookup)

Lookup_value	refers to the compare value, a value that can be entered into the cell or directly in the formula.
Table_array	is the table of values.
Col_index_num	is the number of the column containing the value you are seeking (numbering begins at the first column in the table).

CALCULATIONS

Range_lookup   if entered as FALSE, this looks for an exact match or returns an error.

B14	▼	𝑓ₓ =VLOOKUP(A14,Books,2,FALSE)			
	A	B	C	D	E	F

	A	B	C	D	E	F
11						
12						
13	Book code	Title	Quantity	Sale price	Total	
14	BI02	Light a Penny Candle	1	5.99	5.99	
15	CO03	Cruel and Unusual	2	5.99	11.98	
16	DE06	Way through the Woods	1	5.99	5.99	
17	GR01	Client	1	4.99	4.99	
18	KI03	Green Mile Compilation	1	7.99	7.99	
19						
20						
21				TOTAL AMOUNT DUE	36.94	
22						

In this example, the VLOOKUP function looks for the comparison value (the book code in A14) within another table called "Books" (which is elsewhere on the worksheet). When it finds that code, it moves across the same row to the second column of the "Books" table, where it retrieves the title matching the code.

L- Finding help on a function

▷ **Help - Microsoft Excel Help** or F1

▷ Click the **Table of Contents** link.

▷ In the hierarchy, click **Working with Data**, then **Function Reference**.

▷ Expand one of the function categories and click the function of your choice.

A description of the function appears in a separate window.

If your Internet connection is online, Excel automatically downloads the requested help from the Microsoft web site. If not, a message will tell you that the connection with the server could not be made. Excel will then show you help from the files it keeps on your hard disk.

4.2 Complex calculations

A- Adding statistics to a table

▷ Sort the table by the column containing the entries you want to group together, as a first step to producing a subtotal for each group.

▷ Select the table then choose **Data - Subtotals**.

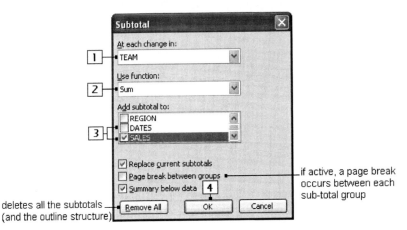

deletes all the subtotals
(and the outline structure)

if active, a page break
occurs between each
sub-total group

1 | Select the column used for grouping.

2 | Choose the type of statistic you require.

3 | Mark the columns containing the values involved in the calculation.

4 | Click to confirm.

1 2 3		A	B	C	D	
	1	TEAM	REGION	DATES	SALES	
	2	Allsopp	South	10-Jan	8,333.00	
	3	Allsopp	Central	17-Jan	2,000.00	
	4	Allsopp	South	17-Jan	8,333.00	
	5	Allsopp Total			18,666.00	
	6	Carter	West	10-Jan	14,167.00	
	7	Carter	West	17-Jan	9,376.00	
	8	Carter Total			23,543.00	
	9	Dickson	North	10-Jan	15,240.00	
	10	Dickson	North	17-Jan	12,250.00	
	11	Dickson	North	24-Jan	1,000.00	
	12	Dickson	East	24-Jan	4,687.00	
	13	Dickson Total			33,177.00	
	14	Harvey	East	10-Jan	9,375.00	
	15	Harvey	East	17-Jan	4,687.00	
	16	Harvey Total			14,062.00	
	17	Lloyd	Central	10-Jan	10,833.00	
	18	Lloyd	West	10-Jan	10,400.00	
	19	Lloyd	Central	17-Jan	8,037.00	
	20	Lloyd	East	24-Jan	4,685.00	
	21	Lloyd Total			33,955.00	
	22	Grand Total			123,403.00	
	23					

Excel calculates the statistics required and constructs an outline.

B - Consolidating worksheets

This technique enables you to combine or analyse values contained in several tables.

▷ Activate the first cell of the range where you want to display the results.

▷ **Data - Consolidate**

CALCULATIONS

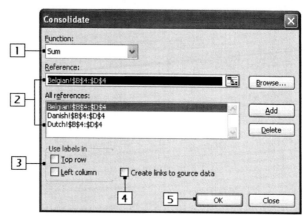

1 | Choose the calculation you want to perform.

2 | For each sheet to be consolidated: activate it and select the cells concerned then click the **Add** button.

3 | If you have included data labels in your selection, indicate where they are located.

4 | If you wish to create a permanent link between the source sheets and the destination sheet, activate this check box.

5 | Click to confirm.

C- Creating a two-input table

| A11 | ▼ | ƒx | =ABS(PMT(D4/12,D5,D3)) |

(this cell contains the calculation formula)   (number of instalments)

	A	B	C	D	E	F	G	H	I	J
2										
3		Capital borrowed		15,000.00						
4		Interest rate		10%						
5		Loan duration in months		12						
6										
7										
8										
9		What are all the possible monthly repayments?								
10		2 years	3 years	4 years	5 years	6 years	7 years	8 years	10 years	
11	1,318.74	24 months	36 months	48 months	60 months	72 months	84 months	96 months	120 months	
12	9.00%	685.27	477.00	373.28	311.38	270.38	241.34	219.75	190.01	
13	9.25%	686.99	478.74	375.06	313.20	272.25	243.24	221.70	192.05	
14	9.50%	688.72	480.49	376.85	315.03	274.12	245.16	223.66	194.10	
15	9.75%	690.44	482.25	378.64	316.86	276.00	247.08	225.63	196.16	
16	10.00%	692.17	484.01	380.44	318.71	277.89	249.02	227.61	198.23	
17										
18										

interest rate   results of the calculation

The table below shows how the amount paid back monthly on a loan varies according to the number of instalments and the interest rate.

▷ In cells located outside the table, enter the initial input values for the calculation (here, D3, D4, and D5).

▷ Enter the variable data, one series in a row, and the other series in a column (row 11, column A).

▷ At the intersection of the row and the column (here, A11) enter the calculation formula, referring to the input cells outside the table.

▷ Select the range of cells including the formula and all the result cells (here A11 to I16).

▷ **Data - Table**

▷ In the **Row input cell** box, indicate which input cell corresponds to the variable data in the row (D5).

▷ In the **Column input cell** box, indicate which input cell formula corresponds to the column data (D4).

▷ Click **OK** to confirm.

D-Calculating with array formulas

This formula allows you to make several calculations giving a single or multiple re-sults. An array formula can only apply to two or more groups of values called array arguments. These arguments must have the same number of rows and columns.

▷ To create an array formula, proceed as for an ordinary calculation, but instead of work-ing on individual cells, work on a selected range of cells and enter using [Ctrl] [⇧ Shift] [Enter], instead of [Enter] or [Ctrl] [Enter].

Here are three examples:

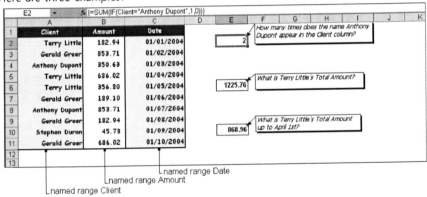

└ named range Date
└ named range Amount
└ named range Client

▷ The array formulas below have been entered in cells E2, E6 and E10:

E2   {=SUM(IF(Client="Anthony Dupont",1,0))}
This formula looks in the range named **Client** for the value **Anthony Du-pont**; if the condition is met, Excel adds **1**, otherwise, Excel adds **0**.

E6   {=SUM(Amount*(Client="Terry Little"))}
This formula calculates the sum of the **Amount** values for **Terry Little**.

E10   {=SUM(Amount*(Client="Terry Little")*(Date<=DATE(2004,4,1)))}
This formula calculates the sum of the amounts for the client **Terry Little**, dated before the **1 April 2004**, inclusively.

You can recognize an array formula by the braces that appear before and after it.

CALCULATIONS

E- Setting a goal value

▷ Activate the cell you wish to set to a certain value and ensure that it contains a calculation formula.

▷ **Tools - Goal Seek**

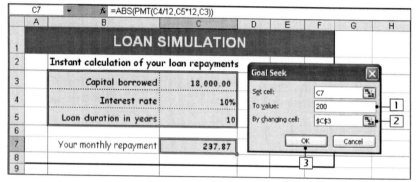

If you only repay 200 a month, how much could you borrow?

1 Enter the value you want to achieve.

2 Give the reference of the cell (or its name if it has one) whose contents should be adjusted.

3 Click to confirm.

As soon as Excel finds a solution, it displays its results on the worksheet.

▷ To accept the result suggested by Excel, click **OK**. The new values are incorporated into the sheet. To return to the original values, click **Cancel**.

F- Making scenarios

A scenario enables you to solve a problem by considering several hypotheses.

Creating scenarios
▷ **Tools - Scenarios**
▷ Click the **Add** button.

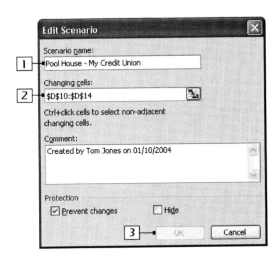

[1] Enter a name for the scenario.

[2] Click and, on the worksheet, select the cells containing the data that will vary.

[3] Click **OK** then enter the values for each changing cell and confirm **OK**.

▷ Create each scenario and click **Close**.

Using a scenario
▷ **Tools - Scenarios**

▷ If you want to run only one scenario, select it then click **Show** (the result replaces the current values on your worksheet).
To run all the scenarios with one action, click the **Summary** button; if necessary, select the cells whose values you want to display for each scenario in the summary sheet; fill in the **Scenario Summary** dialog box and confirm.

The summary is presented as an outline on a separate worksheet.

4.3 Auditing

A-Analysing errors in formulas

Displaying errors

When a cell meant to display a formula result shows an error value such as #NAME?, #N/A, or #DIV/0, it is possible to find all the cells used in the formula.

▷ Activate the cell containing the error message.

▷ Display the **Formula Auditing** toolbar with **Tools - Formula Auditing - Show Formula Auditing Toolbar**.

▷ Click the ⊕ tool button on the **Formula Auditing** toolbar.

F4 ▼	*fx* =E4/E8				
	A	B	C	D	E	F
1						
2		CANADA	GREAT BRITAIN	IRELAND	Total	Average
3	Accountant	1752.00	1763.00	1768.00	5283.00	27%
4	Secretary	1520.00	1532.00	1519.00	45●0	#DIV/0!
5	Warehouse Foreman	1685.00	1701.00	1693.00	5079.00	26%
6	Lorry Driver	1548.00	1562.00	1521.00	4631.00	24%
7	TOTAL				19,864.00	#DIV/0!
8						

The red arrows link the error-causing cell to the cells containing references to it, while the blue arrows show the cell's precedents that caused the error to occur.

Analysing errors in a formula

▷ Use **Tools - Options - Error Checking** tab and check that the **Enable background error checking** option is active and if necessary change the type of errors that Excel should find by activating or deactivating the various **Rules**.

▷ Activate the cell containing the error, indicated by a coloured triangle (green by default) in the upper left corner of the cell.

▷ Click the ⬦ options button at the left of the active cell.

A list of options appears, the first indicating the type of error Excel has found.

	A	B	C	D	E	F	G	H
1								
2		CANADA	GREAT BRITAIN	IRELAND	Total	Average		
3	Accountant	1752.00	1763.00	1768.00	5283.00	27%		
4	Secretary	1520.00	1532.00	1519.00	45	#DIV/0!		
5	Warehouse Foreman	1685.00	1701.00	1693.00	50			
6	Lorry Driver	1548.00	1562.00	1521.00	46	Divide by Zero Error		
7	TOTAL				19,58	Help on this error (a)		
8						Show Calculation Steps... (b)		
9						Ignore Error (c)		
10						Edit in Formula Bar (d)		
11						Error Checking Options... (e)		
12						Show Formula Auditing Toolbar (f)		
13								
14								
15								

F4 ▾ ƒx =E4/E8

▷ Click the option of your choice:

(a)   Displays the help window.

(b)   Shows the **Evaluate Formula** dialog box.

(c)   Turns off the error indicator; the coloured triangle and the options button disappear.

(d)   Positions the insertion point in the formula bar so that you can edit the formula.

(e)   Shows the **Options** dialog box (**Error Checking** tab) so you can choose which **Rules** Excel uses for error checking.

(f)   Displays the **Formula Auditing** toolbar.

Depending on the type of error, other options may be available.

Analysing the errors in all formulas

▷ Activate the worksheet you wish to check for errors.

▷ **Tools**
  Error Checking   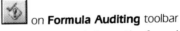 on **Formula Auditing** toolbar

*Excel selects the first cell containing an error and shows the formula and the error in detail in the **Error Checking** dialog box:*

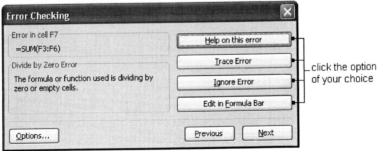

*The buttons on the **Error Checking** dialog box may differ, depending on the type of error.*

▷ Depending on the option you choose, the **Restart** button may appear in the **Error Checking** dialog box which enables you to continue checking the worksheet.

CALCULATIONS

▷ If you wish to go on to the next or previous error without working on the current one, click the **Next** or **Previous** button.

⇨ The **Reset Ignored Errors** button (**Tools - Options - Error Checking** tab) reactivates error indicators in cells where you have chosen the **Ignore Error** option.

B- Evaluating formulas

This technique can be used to see the result of each part of a nested formula.

▷ Select the cell you wish to evaluate.

▷ **Tools**
Formula Auditing
Evaluate Formula

 on the **Formula Auditing** toolbar

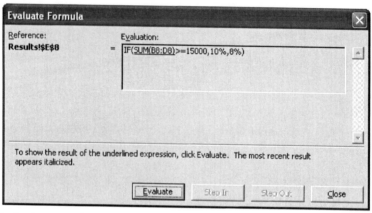

▷ Click **Evaluate** to see the result of the expression underlined in the **Evaluation** box. The result appears within the formula in italics.

▷ Click **Evaluate** again to see the result of the next underlined section and so on.

▷ When you have evaluated the whole formula, click the **Close** button to end the evaluation or the **Restart** button (that replaces the **Evaluate** button) to perform the evaluation again.

⇨ If the formula you are evaluating contains a reference to another formula, the **Step In** button shows the detail of that formula, when it is underlined, in a new part of the evaluation box. The **Step Out** button returns to the initial formula.

C- Tracing the relationships between formulas and cells

▷ To pick out the cells that are involved in a formula, display the precedents: activate the cell containing the formula then use **Tools - Formula Auditing - Trace Precedents** or click 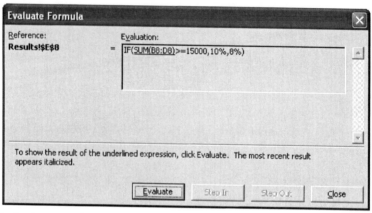 on the **Formula Auditing** toolbar.

▷ To use auditing arrows to find cells that contain formulas that refer to a selected cell, display that cell's dependents:
activate the cell containing the formula then use **Tools - Formula Auditing - Trace Dependents** or click ⊞ on the **Formula Auditing** toolbar.

▷ To clear the auditing arrows, use the **Tools - Formula Auditing - Remove All Arrows** command or the ⊞ tool button (on the **Formula Auditing** toolbar).

CALCULATIONS

5.1 Rows, columns and cells

A- Inserting rows/columns

▷ Select the entire row (or the entire column) after which you wish to insert the new row/column. To insert several rows or columns, select as many rows/columns as you want to insert new ones.

▷ Use **Insert - Rows** or **Columns** or [Ctrl] + or right-click the selection and choose **Insert**.

⇨ *When you insert a row or column, the inserted item adopts the formatting of the row or column previously located there. You can modify this by clicking the **Insert Options** button* 🖌 *that appears next to the inserted item. In the menu that appears, choose to **Format Same As Above** or **Format Same As Below** (for a row), to **Format Same As Right** or **Format Same As Left** (for a column) or to **Clear Formatting** altogether.*

B- Deleting rows/columns

▷ Select the rows (or columns) you wish to delete.

▷ Use **Edit - Delete** or [Ctrl] - or right-click the selection and choose **Delete**.

C- Modifying the width of a column/height of a row

▷ Select each column to be resized to the same width (or each row to be given the same new height); if only one column or row is concerned, you do not need to select it.

▷ Point to the vertical line on the right of one of the selected columns (or to the horizontal line under the row number).

▷ Drag the line to resize the column or row.

⇨ *You can adjust the width of a column or the height of a row to fit its widest or tallest cell entry. To do this, double-click the vertical line to the right of the letter, to adjust the width of a column, or double-click the horizontal line beneath the number, to adjust the height of a row.*

D- Moving and inserting cells/rows/columns

▷ Select the cells, rows or columns to be moved.

▷ Point to one edge of the selected range then holding the [⇧ Shift] key down, drag the selection into position.

▷ Release the mouse when the insertion point (displayed as a thick grey line) is correctly placed.

Excel moves the cells (or rows or columns), inserting them between the existing cells (or rows or columns).

⇨ *Holding down [Ctrl] as well as [⇧ Shift] when you drag a selection moves a copy of the cells, rows or columns instead of the original item.*

E- Inserting/deleting cells

▷ Select as many cells as you are going to insert.

▷ **Insert - Cells**
or right-click the selection and choose **Insert**.

indicate what you want
to do with the cells
already in place

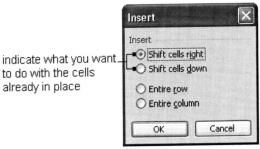

⇨ To delete the selected cells, use **Edit - Delete** then choose to **Shift cells left** or to **Shift cells up**.

F- Creating and using an outline

An outline is a way of viewing or printing the main results of a table, without looking at unnecessary detail.

▷ To create an outline manually, select the rows (or columns) that will be part of the same outline level and use **Data - Group and Outline - Group**.

▷ To create an automatic outline, select the table concerned and use **Data - Group and Outline - Auto Outline**.

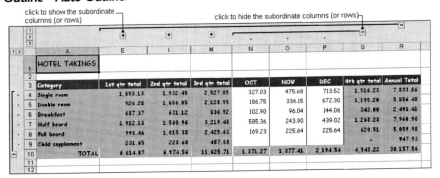

▷ To insert a column/row into the previous level group, select the column/row and use **Data - Group and Outline - Group**.

▷ To remove a column/row from a group, select the column/row and use **Data - Group and Outline - Ungroup**.

⇨ To remove an outline, select the table concerned and use **Data - Group and Outline - Clear Outline**.

5.2 Formatting

A- Applying an automatic format to a table

▷ Select the table to be formatted then use **Format - AutoFormat**.

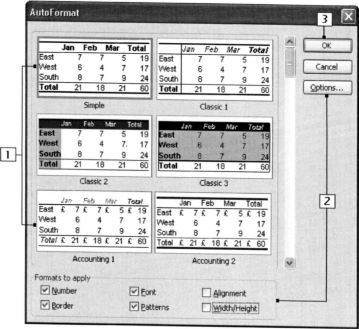

1 Select the format.

2 Click **Options** to display and customise the **Formats to apply**.

3 Apply the format.

B- Formatting numerical values

▷ Select the cells concerned then choose one of the number formats from the **Formatting** toolbar:

Currency	(£10,000.00/$10,000.00 etc)
Euro	(€ 10,000.00)
Percent Style	(1000000%)
Comma Style	(10,000.00)

⇨ *Hash symbols (#) may appear if a cell's width is insufficient; increase the column width, as necessary.*

⇨ *If you use Windows XP, you can change the default currency settings using the Windows **start** menu - **Control Panel - Regional and Language Options** (or **Date, Time, Language**, and **Regional Options**, depending on your view) - **Customize** button (or choose a task from the list).*

⇨ *If necessary, click the* 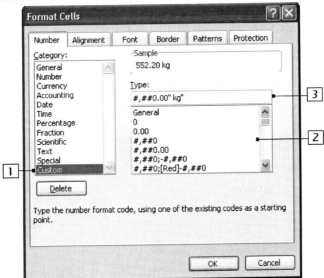 *tool button to show one more decimal place or* *to show one less. Other formats are available in the **Format Cells** dialog box (**Format - Cells**).*

⇨ *You can display monetary values converted into Euros and vice versa. Display the **EuroValue** toolbar (install the **Euro Currency Tools** add-in if you do not find this bar), open the* `Off ▾` *list and select the type of conversion you want to make. Next, click a cell to see its converted value in the first text box on the **EuroValue** toolbar.*

C - Formatting dates and times

▷ Select the cells containing the dates or times.
▷ **Format - Cells** or Ctrl 1 - **Number** tab
▷ Choose the **Date** or **Time Category**.
▷ Click the required format in the **Type** list.

D - Creating a custom format

▷ Select the cells to which you want to apply the format.
▷ **Format - Cells** or Ctrl 1 - **Number** tab

1 Select the **Custom** category.

Excel 2003

2 Choose the format closest to what you have in mind.

3 Enter your custom format.

⇨ *When text is being added to a format, it must be entered between quotation marks.*

⇨ *Use the @ character to represent the cell contents, when the cell contains text.*

⇨ *For hiding cell contents, create a ;;; (three semi-colons) format.*

E - Creating a conditional format

▷ Select the cells concerned.
▷ **Format - Conditional Formatting**

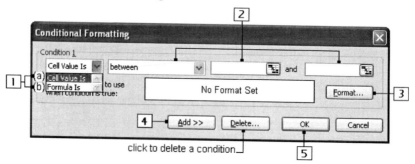

click to delete a condition

1 Indicate whether:
   (a)   the condition applies to a value contained in the selected cells
   (b)   the condition applies to a formula.

2 If you have chosen (a), select an operator of comparison and the compare values. If you have chosen (b), give the formula.

3 Define the format which will be applied to the cells if the condition is met then click **OK** in the **Format Cells** dialog box.

4 Define additional formats if you need to.

5 Create the format(s).

F - Modifying the orientation of a text

▷ Select the cells concerned.
▷ **Format - Cells** or Ctrl 1

▷ Under the **Alignment** tab, choose **Orientation**:

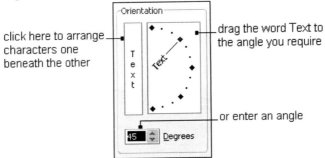

click here to arrange characters one beneath the other

drag the word Text to the angle you require

or enter an angle

G-Aligning cell contents

▷ Select the cells concerned then click  left alignment, centred or right alignment.

▷ **Format - Cells** or [Ctrl] **1** - **Alignment** tab

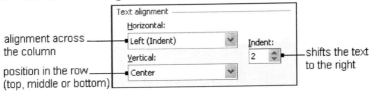

alignment across the column

position in the row (top, middle or bottom)

shifts the text to the right

⇨ To indent cell contents, choose **Left (Indent)** or **Right (Indent)** in the **Horizontal** alignment, depending on where the indent should start, and then give the **Indent** value in the text box, each increment representing one character width. The 🔲 and 🔲 tool buttons on the **Formatting** toolbar respectively increase and decrease the left indent.

⇨ To centre cell contents across several columns, select the cells across which the text should be centred (the first cell in the range must contain the text) and click 🔲. This centres the text and merges the cells. To undo the cell merge, click this tool button again.

H-Modifying the font/size/colour of the characters

▷ Select the cells or characters concerned then choose the font, size and colour from the list boxes on the **Formatting** toolbar.

	C	D	E	F
	FEBRUARY	**MARCH**		
	3,958.00	4,578.50		
	3,250.00	2,356.00		
	3,845.00	4,578.90		
	7,890.00	7,845.10		
	4,560.00	3,589.00		
	7,125.00	4,560.00		
8 BEN	3,875.00	4,500.00	5,230.00	
9 PHILIP	4,580.00	5,845.00	2,356.00	
10				

font-size list boxes:
- Sylfaen
- Symbol ΑβΧδΕφΓηΙφ
- System
- Tahoma
- Tempus Sans ITC
- Terminal
- Times New Roman
- Times New Roman MT Extra I
- Trebuchet MS
- Tunga
- Verdana
- Vivaldi

⇨ If the cell contents cannot be seen in their entirety, you can adjust the character size automatically to fit the cell using **Format - Cells - Alignment** tab and ticking the **Shrink to fit** option.

⇨ To redefine the default font and font size used in a workbook, use **Tools - Options - General** tab. Define the new **Standard font** and **Size**. These modifications will take effect when you next start Excel.

I- Formatting characters

▷ Select the cells or characters concerned then activate the attribute(s) you want to apply:

B	Ctrl B	**bold**
I	Ctrl I	*Italic*
U	Ctrl U	underlined

⇨ If you repeat the same action for the same text, you cancel the corresponding attribute.

⊞▷ Select the cells or characters concerned then use **Format** - **Cells** or ⌨Ctrl⌨ 1 - **Font** tab.

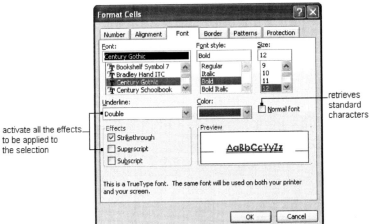

activate all the effects
to be applied to
the selection

retrieves
standard
characters

J- Drawing borders around cells

Applying predefined borders

✍▷ Select the cells concerned then choose a border from the ▦▾ palette on the **Formatting** toolbar:

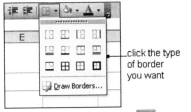

click the type
of border
you want

⊞▷ Select the cells concerned and use **Format** - **Cells** or ⌨Ctrl⌨ 1 - **Border** tab.

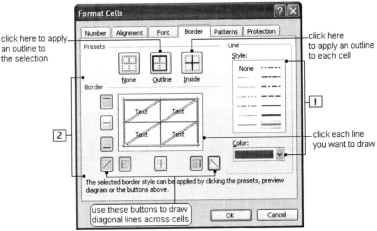

click here to apply
an outline to
the selection

click here
to apply an outline
to each cell

click each line
you want to draw

use these buttons to draw
diagonal lines across cells

Excel 2003   **57**

1 Choose a style and a colour.

2 Indicate the position of the lines making up the border.

Drawing borders

▷ Open the 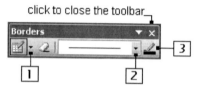 list by clicking the black arrow then click the **Draw Borders** option.

*The **Borders** toolbar appears and the pointer takes the shape of a pencil. The default drawing mode is **Draw Border** which draws an outline around the selected area.*

click to close the toolbar

1 If you wish to draw inside gridlines instead, open this list and choose the **Draw Border Grid** option. When you choose this mode, the pencil pointer is accompanied by a small grid.

2 If required, open this list and choose a line style.

3 Click if you want to select another colour.

▷ To draw a border along one edge of a range of cells, drag along that edge.

▷ To draw a border around the outside of a range or a grid within a range, drag from the starting cell up to the last cell required.

▷ To remove one or more borders, click the [ ] tool button (the pointer becomes an eraser) and drag along the borders you wish to erase.

▷ To deactivate the border drawing mode, press Esc or click [ ] or [ ] again.

⇨ *While you are using **Draw Border** mode, you can temporarily switch to **Draw Border Grid** mode by holding down the Ctrl key. Holding down the ⇧Shift key switches to erasing mode, with the pointer becoming an eraser temporarily.*

K- Applying colour/patterns to cells

▷ Select the cells that you want to colour then open the [ ] list and choose a colour.

⇨ *A click on the [ ] tool button applies the last colour used.*

▷ Select the cells that you want to colour or shade then use **Format - Cells** or Ctrl 1 - **Patterns** tab.

▷ Choose a **Color** and a **Pattern**.

L- Merging cells

▷ Select the cells that you want to combine into a single cell (only the data in the first cell of the selection will appear in the merged cells).

▷ **Format - Cells** or Ctrl 1 - **Alignment** tab

▷ Tick the **Merge cells** option and confirm.

⇨ *The* [icon] *tool button merges selected cells and centres the data horizontally in the merged cells.*

5.3 Styles and templates

A- Creating a style

A style is a way of saving a collection of attributes that you can then apply to other cells more quickly.

▷ Activate the cell whose formatting is to be saved as a style.

▷ **Format - Style** or [Alt] ′

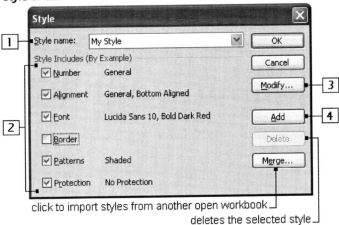

```
click to import styles from another open workbook ┘
                                deletes the selected style ┘
```

[1] Give a name for the new style.

[2] Deactivate any attributes you do not require.

[3] If you need to, make changes to the formatting.

[4] Create the style.

B- Applying a style

▷ Select the cells to be formatted.

▷ **Format - Style** or [Alt] ′

▷ Select the style you want to use in the **Style name** list and click **OK**.

C- Creating a template

▷ Set up the workbook template, adding any elements you want workbooks created from this template to have. If required, activate worksheet or cell protection.

▷ **File - Save As**

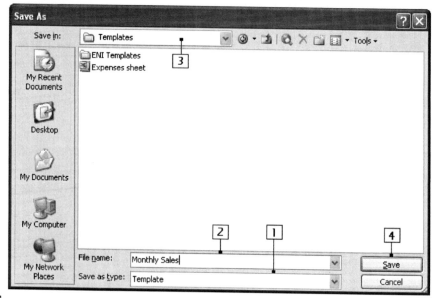

1 Choose the **Template** option.

2 Give the new template a name.

3 If necessary, select another folder or a subfolder of **Templates**.

4 Save the template.

⇨ Template files have an .XLT extension.

⇨ To open a template, proceed as for any other workbook, but remember to select **Templates** in the **Files of type** list in the **Open** dialog box. As a rule, when saved on your hard disk, templates are saved in C:\Documents and Settings\user_name\ Application Data\Microsoft\Templates.

6.1 Printing

A- Printing a sheet/a workbook

▷ To print a sheet using the active page setup settings, activate the sheet in question and click the ![tool] tool button.

▷ To define specific printing options, use **File - Print** or Ctrl **P**.

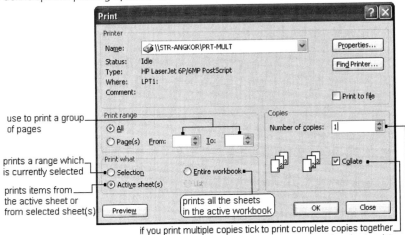

⇨ If what you are printing is several pages wide or high, you can choose how to print these pages by using the **Down, then over** or **Over, then down** options in the **Page order** frame in **File - Page Setup - Sheet** tab.

B- Creating a print area

You can define the part of the sheet you want to print as a print area.

▷ Select the range to be printed.

▷ **File - Print Area - Set Print Area**

⇨ Excel keeps the last print area created in memory. To delete the print area, use **File - Print Area - Clear Print Area**.

C- Managing page breaks

▷ Activate the cell which is going to be the first of your new page.

▷ **Insert - Page Break**

The page break is represented by a dotted line.

⇨ To delete the page break, activate a cell in the next row or column and use **Insert - Remove Page Break**.

⇨ *The* **View - Page Break Preview** *command makes the page breaks visible as blue lines on the worksheet, which you can move by dragging.*

D-Repeating titles on each page

▷ **File - Page Setup - Sheet** tab

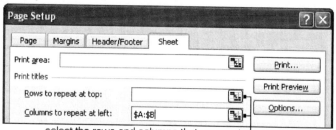

> select the rows and columns that you want to print on each page

In this example, columns A and B will print on each page.

E- Displaying the Print Preview

▷ **File - Print Preview** or

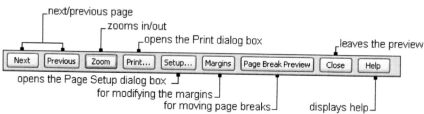

▷ To zoom in on a preview, place the mouse pointer on the item to be magnified and click. Click again to return to a smaller scale.

▷ To change the width of margins and columns widths, click the **Margins** button and drag the appropriate handle:

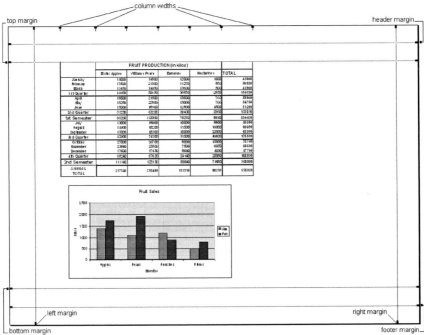

6.2 Page setup

A - Modifying page setup options

▷ **File - Page Setup** or click the **Setup** button in the Print Preview.

▷ Activate the **Margins** tab to define the margins.

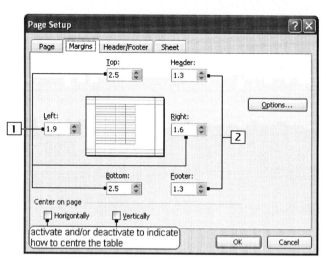

$\boxed{1}$ Set the margins for printing.

$\boxed{2}$ Set the positions of the header and footer.

▷ To modify the **Scaling** options, click the **Page** tab:

choose the page orientation

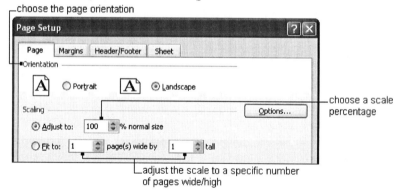

choose a scale percentage

adjust the scale to a specific number of pages wide/high

▷ Set the **Print** options under the **Sheet** tab:

prints the row numbers and the column letters

prints or omits the sheet grid

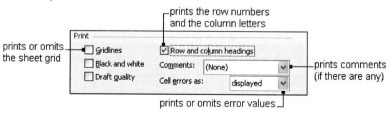

prints comments (if there are any)

prints or omits error values

B - Creating headers and footers

▷ **File - Page Setup** or click the **Setup** button in the Print Preview - **Header/Footer** tab; you could also use the command **View - Header/Footer**.

▷ Choose a predefined **Header** or **Footer** in the lists, or click the **Custom Header** or **Custom Footer** button in the **Page Setup** dialog box.

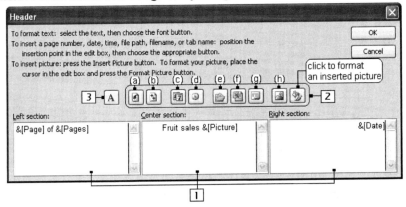

☐1 Enter the text to be printed in the box which corresponds to the position on the page where you want the header/footer to appear. To create a second (third...) line of text, press [Enter].

☐2 To insert variable details click the appropriate buttons.

(a)	Page number	(e)	Workbook name and file path
(b)	Total number of pages	(f)	Name of the workbook
(c)	Date of printing	(g)	Name of the sheet
(d)	Time of printing	(h)	Picture

☐3 Format the text you select in one of the boxes.

C-Working with views

A view is a way of saving certain settings, such as a print area, page setup, filter settings or hidden rows/columns. When you switch to a view, the saved options are activated automatically.

▷ To create a view, prepare the sheet for printing (page setup, print area, hiding columns, etc), and use **View - Custom Views - Add**

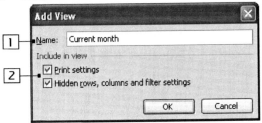

☐1 Enter the name of the view being created.

☐2 Indicate the elements which should be included in the view.

▷ To use a view, take **View - Custom Views** and double-click the view you want to activate.

Excel 2003

PRINTING

7.1 Creating a chart

A - Creating a chart

▷ Select the cells that contain the data needed for the chart.

If the data for the chart is in several different ranges, select the non-adjacent ranges in the usual way (with Ctrl *-clicks). Make sure the cell ranges selected form a coherent set each time, including blank cells if necessary.*

	A	B	C	D
1		JANUARY	FEBRUARY	MARCH
2	PETER	4,568.90	3,958.00	4,578.50
3	CALLUM	2,587.00	3,250.00	2,356.00
4	SUE	6,589.10	3,845.00	4,578.90
5	JOSH	6,348.00	7,890.00	7,845.10
6	ANNE	2,890.00	4,560.00	3,589.00
7	WENDY	4,578.90	7,125.00	4,560.00
8	BEN	3,875.00	4,500.00	5,230.00
9	PHILIP	4,580.00	5,845.00	2,356.00

Excel considers the selected ranges as one rectangular block →

	A	C
		FEBRUARY
	PETER	3,958.00
	CALLUM	3,250.00
	ANNE	4,560.00
	WENDY	7,125.00

In the example above, the blank cell in the top left corner was included to ensure a symmetrical selection.

▷ **Insert - Chart** or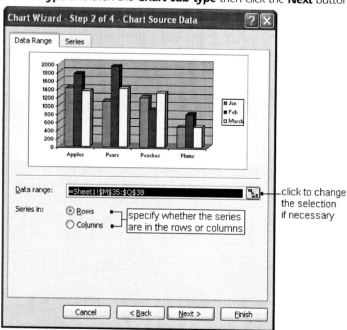

▷ Select the **Chart type** and then the **Chart sub-type** then click the **Next** button.

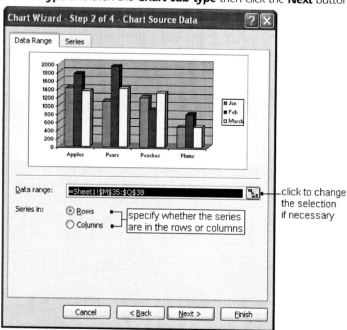

▷ If the chart shown does not resemble the required chart, click the **Series** tab to check the references of each series. In the list, select a **Series** and check and edit if necessary the **Name** and the **Values** of the cell references making up each series. Also check, and edit if required, the **Category (X) axis labels**, then click the **Next** button.

▷ Customise your chart by giving the various chart titles on the **Titles** page. At this stage in the wizard, you can also select options from the other tabs; click **Next**.

where do you want to put the chart ?

▷ Click **Finish**.

⇨ In you chose to insert the chart into a worksheet, it appears in the workspace. Square black handles show that it is selected. This type of chart is known as an *embedded chart*.

⇨ When an embedded chart (created from adjacent data) is selected, the matching cell ranges appear with colour coding; series are in a green rectangle, categories in a purple rectangle and data points in a blue rectangle.

⇨ To activate an embedded chart, click it once to select it or one of its parts (the **Data** menu is replaced by the **Chart** menu). To deactivate it, click a cell in the sheet, outside the chart.

⇨ To move an embedded chart, activate it then drag it to its new position.

⇨ To redefine the chart's data, use the **Chart - Source Data** command: under **Data Range** you can redefine the source range of cells, and under **Series**, you can redefine the contents of the **Names**, **Values** and **Category (X) axis labels**.

B - Selecting different objects in a chart

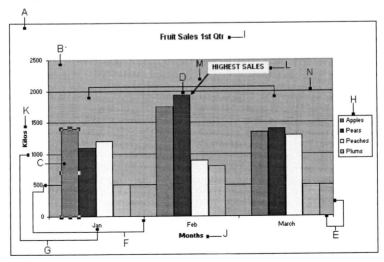

A	Chart area	H	Series legend
B	Plot area	I	Chart title
C	Point	J	Value axis title
D	Series	K	Category axis title
E	Value axis/Category axis	L	Text box
F	Tick marks	M	Drawing object
G	Tick mark labels	N	Gridlines

▷ To select any item, click it or open the **Chart Objects** list on the **Chart** toolbar and click its name. To select a point, click the series first and then the point.

▷ To resize or remove an object, select it and drag one of its selection handles to resize it or drag it by its edges to move it.

▷ To delete a selected item, press ⌷Del⌷ or use **Edit - Clear - All**.

⇨ *When you point to a chart object, its name and if appropriate, its value appear in a ScreenTip, providing the **Show names** and **Show values** options are active in the **Options** dialog box (**Tools - Options - Chart** tab).*

⇨ *To access a dialog box in which you can format a chart object, select the object then use the first command in the **Format** menu. This command name changes depending on the object. You can also double-click the selected item.*

C - Setting up the chart for printing

▷ Select the chart.

▷ **File - Page Setup**

▷ As well as modifying the usual options, you can adjust the **Printed chart size** under the **Chart** tab.

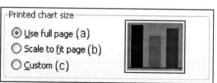

(a) Changes the chart's proportions so it takes up the whole page.

(b) Increases the chart's size so it prints on the page, without affecting its proportions.

(c) Prints the chart according to the actual object's size.

7.2 Chart options

A- Changing the chart type

▷ To change the type of all the series in the chart, just activate the chart; to change the type of one specific series, select that series.

▷ **Chart - Chart Type**

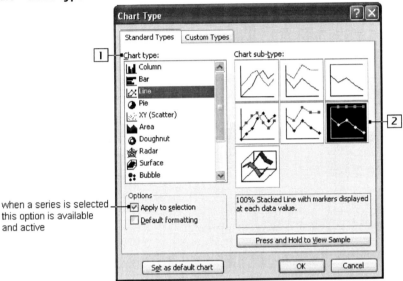

1 Choose the chart type.

2 Double-click the sub-type you prefer.

⇨ You can use the ▨▾ button on the **Chart** toolbar to change the chart type but not to choose from the various sub-types.

⇨ All the options for managing the chart can be found in **Chart - Chart Options**.

B- Creating a custom chart

▷ Select the chart on which you want to base your custom chart.

▷ **Chart - Chart Type - Custom Types** tab

▷ Activate the **User-defined** option under **Select from** and click the **Add** button.

▷ Fill in the **Add Custom Chart Type** dialog box with the chart's **Name** and its **Description**.

▷ Click **OK** on both dialog boxes.

C- Using a custom chart

▷ Select the data you want to represent in a chart.

▷ **Insert - Chart - Custom Types** tab

▷ Activate the **User-defined** option under **Select from**.

▷ Double-click the required **Chart type**.

▷ Type the references of the data you want the chart to represent in the **Data range** frame or modify the selection, then specify if the data series are in **Rows** or **Columns**.

▷ Click **Next**.

▷ Give the **Chart title** and the axes titles under the **Titles** tab and, if necessary, set the various display options from the chart under the other tabs.

▷ Click the **Next** button.

▷ Choose where you want to create the chart and click **Finish**.

D- Displaying the data table

Under the chart, you can display the table of data on which it is based.

▷ Click the button on the **Chart** toolbar or use **Chart - Chart Options - Data Table** tab and activate the **Show data table** option.

E- Inserting gridlines in a chart

▷ **Chart - Chart Options - Gridlines** tab

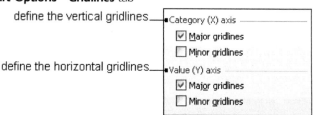

define the vertical gridlines ⎯⎯ Category (X) axis
  ☑ Major gridlines
  ☐ Minor gridlines
define the horizontal gridlines ⎯⎯ Value (Y) axis
  ☑ Major gridlines
  ☐ Minor gridlines

F- Changing the scale of the chart

▷ Select the value axis.

▷ **Format**
  Selected Axis
  Scale tab

Ctrl 1

▷ Set the scale options:

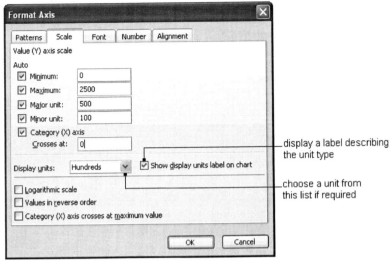

display a label describing the unit type

choose a unit from this list if required

G-Modifying the display of tick marks and their labels

▷ Select the axis on which the tick mark labels need formatting.

▷ **Format**   Ctrl 1
  Selected Axis

for formatting the text in the labels

for formatting numbers in the labels

for orienting the text in the labels

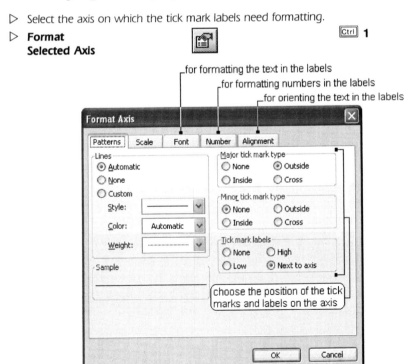

choose the position of the tick marks and labels on the axis

CHARTS AND OBJECTS

⇨ With the 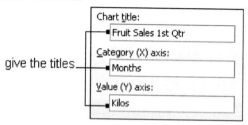 and buttons on the **Chart** toolbar you can also change the orientation of the text in the labels.

H-Adding text to a chart

A title

▷ **Chart - Chart Options - Titles** tab

give the titles———

A text linked to one or more points in a series

▷ Select the point or series concerned.

▷ **Format**
Selected Data
or **Selected Data Series** - **Data Labels** tab

Ctrl 1

1 Activate the options of your choice.

2 If you choose several options, select the type of separator to display between each value.

Unattached text (text box)

▷ Make sure that you have not selected any text objects.

▷ Type the text required and press Enter .

The drawing object created is named Text Box. It is placed in the middle of the chart and can be moved like a drawing object.

⇨ *To enter different types of text on several lines, press* Ctrl Enter *every time you change lines.*

The contents of a cell in the sheet

▷ Make sure that you have not selected any chart object containing text.

▷ Type **=**

▷ Select the cell(s) containing the text to be inserted and enter.

▷ Drag the text box to where you want it.

⇨ *Each time the contents of the cells from the worksheet change, this text will be updated.*

⇨ *To edit the contents of a text object, select it, click in the text, make your changes and press* ⌷Esc⌷.

I- Managing the legend

▷ If necessary, activate the chart then use **Chart - Chart Options - Legend** tab.

▷ To display or hide the legend, activate or deactivate the **Show legend** option.

▷ If required, choose the legend's **Placement** (position) in relation to the chart.

▷ Click **OK**.

⇨ *You can also show or hide the legend with the* ▨ *tool button on the* **Chart** *toolbar.*

⇨ *The legend can also be dragged to its new position.*

J- Formatting a chart object's text

▷ Select the chart object that contains the text.

▷ Use the tools on the **Formatting** toolbar or click the ▨ tool button on the **Chart** toolbar to set the formatting attributes.

⇨ *You can also do this to format numerical values.*

K- Changing the border/colour/shading of a chart object

▷ Select the element you want to modify.

▷ **Format Selected [object]**   double-click the object   ⌷Ctrl⌷ **1**

▷ If necessary, activate the **Patterns** tab.

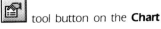

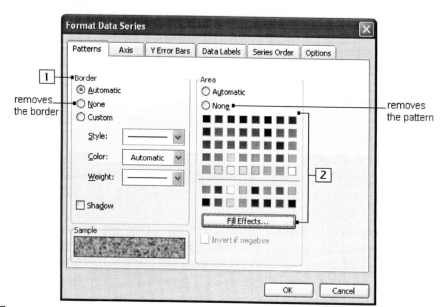

Choose a border.

② Choose a background colour, pattern or texture.

⇨ To add a simple colour, select the item and use [icon].

L- Adding/deleting a category in an embedded chart

▷ Select the chart area.

🖱▷ To add a new category and its corresponding data points, drag the handle of the purple rectangle until it encompasses the cells containing the new category. To delete a category, reduce the rectangle so the data in question is excluded from it.

⇨ If the category you wish to add is not adjacent to the existing categories, you can select the corresponding cells and drag them into the chart.

▷ Select the chart area then use **Chart - Add Data**.

▷ In the **Range** text box, give the references of the data you want to add then click **OK**.

▷ If the **Paste Special** dialog box appears, activate the **New point(s)** option. In the **Values (Y) in** frame, indicate whether the series are in rows or columns. Activate the **Categories (X Labels) in First Column** (or **Row**) option if the selected range contains category labels.

▷ Click **OK**.

M -Adding a secondary axis

If the values of several series vary greatly or if the series represent different types of data (for example sales and their distribution as a percentage), you could represent one or more series on a second axis.

▷ Select the series concerned then choose **Format - Selected Data Series - Axis** tab.

▷ Activate the **Secondary axis** option then click **OK**.

N -Managing data series

▷ To add a data series select the chart area (the cells containing the data series are enclosed in a green rectangle) and drag the handle of the green rectangle until it has encompassed the values of the new series. If the chart is in a chart sheet, you can copy the source data using the clipboard.

▷ To delete a data series, choose **Chart - Source Data - Series** tab, select the **Series** and click the **Remove** button.

▷ To modify the order of the series, select one of the chart's series and use **Format -**

Selected Data Series - Series Order tab or [icon] or Ctrl 1.

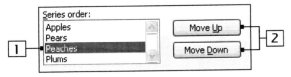

1 Click the series you wish to move.

2 Click one of these buttons to move the series up or down the order.

O -Managing pie charts

▷ To rotate a pie chart, select the series then use:

Format
Selected Data Series
Options tab

Ctrl 1

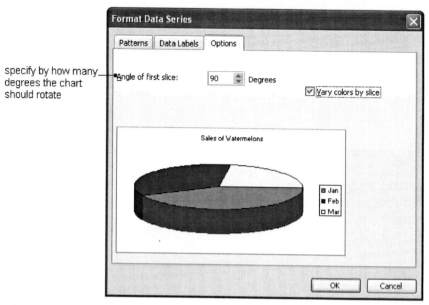

specify by how many degrees the chart should rotate

▷ To "explode" a slice of the pie (move it out from the chart), select the slice you want to move and drag it outwards.

P- Linking points in a line chart

▷ Select a series.

▷ **Format**
Selected Data Series
Options tab

[Ctrl] 1

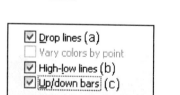

▷ Choose between:

(a)	the line starts from the highest point and finishes on the category axis.
(b)	the line links the highest and the lowest value for each category.
(c)	the points are linked by bars instead of lines.

Q-Changing the display of a 3-D chart

▷ **Chart - 3-D View**

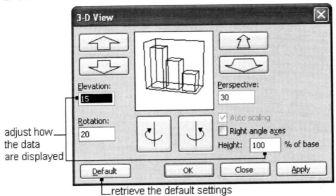

adjust how the data are displayed

retrieve the default settings

▷ To change the depth of a series in a 3-D chart, select the series concerned and use **Format - Selected Data Series - Options** tab; in the **Chart depth** box, enter a depth percentage in relation to the width.

R- Unlinking a chart from the worksheet

▷ For each data series:
- select the series,
- select everything that appears in the formula bar,
- press  F9 and enter.

7.3 Drawing objects

A- Drawing an object

▷ Display the **Drawing** toolbar.

▷ Click the tool button corresponding to the shape you want to draw or click the **AutoShapes** button then choose one of the shapes proposed.

▷ Click to draw an object of a preset size or drag on the workspace to draw the object. Hold down Alt as you drag to align the object with the cell gridlines.

▷ If the drawing object (AutoShape or text box) can contain text, start to type the text without worrying about the line breaks, using Enter when you want to create a new paragraph; press Esc to confirm your finished text.

⇨ Hold the ⌐⇧ Shift⌐ key down to draw a perfect circle, square or arc, and for a perfectly straight horizontal, vertical or diagonal line.

⇨ You can go on to format the characters you have entered.

⇨ To add text to a drawing or AutoShape, right-click the drawn shape and select **Add Text**.

B- Inserting a picture, a sound or a video clip

▷ Display the **Clip Art** task pane (**Insert - Picture - Clip Art**).

If the **Add clips to Organizer** dialog box appears, click the **Now** button if you want to add the image, audio and video files from your hard disk or another source into the Clip Organizer (if you do not want to do that just yet, click the **Later** button).

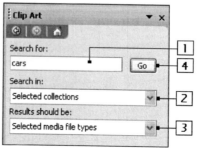

1 Enter one or more keywords for your search.

2 Define where the search should be carried out by selecting (or deselecting) the corresponding categories.

The **Office Collections** category and its subcategories correspond to the image, sound and video elements installed with Office. The **Web Collections** category provides you with elements found on the Web (or more precisely on the Microsoft site). Excel will take this category into account only if you have an open Internet connection.

3 If necessary, limit the type of items included in the search (**Clip Art**, **Photographs**, **Movies** or **Sounds**), by selecting or deselecting these elements as required.

4 Start the search.

If you want to interrupt the search, click the **Stop** button that replaces **Go**.

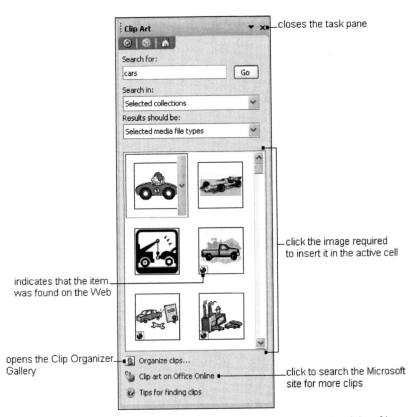

closes the task pane

click the image required to insert it in the active cell

indicates that the item was found on the Web

opens the Clip Organizer Gallery

click to search the Microsoft site for more clips

▷ To work with an item, point to it and click the arrow that appears to the right of it.

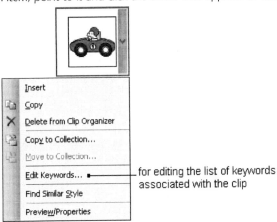

for editing the list of keywords associated with the clip

⇨ *To see more complex AutoShapes in the **Insert Clip Art** task pane, click the **Auto-Shapes** button on the **Drawing** toolbar and choose the **More AutoShapes** option.*

⇨ *To display an image in the background of a worksheet, activate the sheet then use **Format - Sheet - Background**, choose the image then click **Insert**.*

CHARTS AND OBJECTS

C- Modifying a picture

▷ To change the size of a selected picture, use **Format - Picture - Size** tab and under **Size and rotate** enter a new **Height** and **Width**.

▷ To modify a picture's colours, select it and use the tools on the **Picture** toolbar.

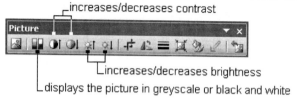

```
                    ┌─increases/decreases contrast
```
```
                          └increases/decreases brightness
        └displays the picture in greyscale or black and white
```

▷ To crop a picture, select the picture concerned and click .

To crop one side, point to the middle cropping handle on that side, then when the pointer takes the shape of a "T", drag into the picture.

To crop two opposing sides or four sides simultaneously, hold down Ctrl, then drag one of the corresponding middle or corner cropping handles towards the centre of the picture.

To end the cropping process, click the [🔳] tool button again.

D- Inserting a WordArt object

The WordArt application applies special effects to a text:

▷ Click the [◢] button on the **Drawing** toolbar.

▷ Select an effect then click **OK**.

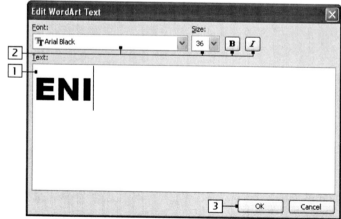

1 Type in the text (use Enter for a new paragraph).

2 Format the text, if appropriate.

3 Create the object.

⇨ *When the text object is selected, you can edit it using the tools from the **WordArt** bar.*

E - Inserting a diagram

▷ Click the 🔲 tool button on the **Drawing** toolbar.

▷ Select the type of diagram you wish to use then click **OK**.

*The chosen type of diagram appears on the sheet and the **Organization Chart** toolbar appears, if you choose that type of diagram. If you choose another type, the **Diagram** toolbar appears.*

▷ Enter your text in the **Click to add text** boxes.

▷ To add another shape to an **Organization Chart**, choose the shape to which you wish to link the new one. Open the **Insert Shape** list on the **Organization Chart** toolbar and select the type of shape you wish to add. For other types of diagram, just click the **Insert Shape** button on the **Diagram** toolbar.

▷ To delete a shape from a diagram, click the edge of the shape to select it, then press ⌊Del⌋.

⇨ *The 🔲 tool button on the **Organization Chart** or **Diagram** toolbar applies an automatic format to the diagram.*

⇨ *To delete a diagram, click it to activate it then click its hatched border and press ⌊Del⌋*

F - Managing drawing objects

▷ Click 🔲 on the **Drawing** toolbar.

▷ To select several objects at once, click the first object to select it and hold down the ⌊⇧ Shift⌋ key as you click each of the other objects you want to select.

▷ To delete an object, select it and press ⌊Del⌋.

▷ To resize an object, drag one of the handles which surround it when it is selected.

▷ To move an object, point to its border and drag it. Use the ⌊Alt⌋ key as you drag to align the object with the cell grid.

▷ To group a collection of selected objects, click the **Draw** button on the **Drawing** toolbar, then click **Group**. To ungroup objects, use **Draw - Ungroup**.

▷ To change the order of overlapping objects, select the object that you want to bring forward or send further back. Click the **Draw** button then point to the **Order** option.

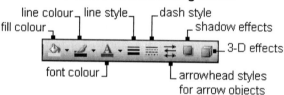

Choose:

(a)/(b)   to bring the object to the front/to send the object to the back.

(c)/(d)   to bring it one place forward/to send it one place back.

▷ To align objects with one another, select the objects concerned, click the **Draw** button then choose one of the first six options in the **Align or Distribute** menu.

▷ To rotate an object, select it then point to the small green circle at the top of the object or picture and drag to rotate the object.

G-Changing an object's appearance

A 2-D object

▷ Select the object and use the buttons on the **Drawing** toolbar:

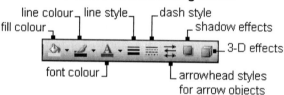

⇨ *To remove an object's borders, select it then open the* list *and choose* **No Line***.*

A 3-D object

▷ To add a 3-D effect to an object, select the object then click the button on the **Drawing** toolbar to choose a preset 3-D style.

To create your own 3-D effect, select the object, click then the **3-D Settings** button.

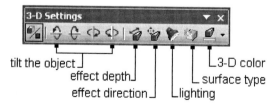

8.1 Lists

A- Creating a list

Excel provides you with convenient features to help you manage and analyse lists of related data. You can define several ranges as lists on the same worksheet.

▷ Select the range of cells that you want to convert into a list.

▷ **Data - List - Create List** or ⌨ **L**

1 Tick this option is there are already headers on the range of data.

2 Click to create the list.

drop-down
Autofilter lists

displays/hides a row
of totals after
the insert row

insert row

	A	B	C	D	E	F	G	H	I
1	Surname	First Name	Address	PC/City	Sex	Age	Subs	Paid	
2	Alderman	Christine	56 Harvey St	4100 Tewesbury	F	13	2.50	Y	
3	Barnett	Frances	38 Harrison Cres	4500 Greerton	F	15	3.00	N	
4	Blake	Peter	35 Nichol St	5500 Killybill	M	18	4.50	Y	
5	Charles	Yolanda	29 Bartlett Cres	6000 Lorton	F	14	3.00	Y	
6	Cray	Hannah	77 Kennedy Drive	5800 Rafter	F	17	4.50	Y	
7	Dall	Tammy	13 Read Road	4300 Dryden	F	16	4.50	Y	
8	Dorcas	Michelle	10 Kings Ct	5400 Fern Grove	F	16	4.50	Y	
9	Evans	Michael	35 Prior St	6300 Stoughton	M	33	8.00	Y	
10	Grant	Jessica	14/196 Red Sand Road	6100 Herston	F	17	4.50	N	
11	Grey	Josephine	89 Green St	5500 Killybill	F	22	8.00	N	
12	Hunt	Rosemary	32 Fern Drive	5000 Gunston	F	18	4.50	Y	
13	Jones	Andrew	19 Playton Place	4000 Westport	M	19	8.00	N	
14	Junger	Karl	4 Broadway	4300 Dryden	M	19	8.00	Y	
15	Kelsey	Ross					8.00	Y	
16	Layton	Campbell					8.00	Y	
17	Lindell	Norman					8.00	Y	
18	Lindstrom	Ian	86 Clarence St	6200 Ipswich	M	26	8.00	Y	
19	Marsh	Sarah	19 River Lane	6000 Lorton	F	19	8.00	Y	
20	Norton	Vera	18 Quinn St	4100 Tewesbury	F	24	8.00	Y	
21	O Brian	Sean	45 Lincoln St	4100 Tewesbury	M	19	8.00	N	
22	Peak	Alison	26A Pine Road	4200 New Grove	F	21	8.00	Y	
23	Richards	Brendan	32 Yarmouth Ave	4000 Westport	M	25	8.00	Y	
24	Salakis	Alex	85 Kessler Ave	6200 Ipswich	M	15	3.00	N	
25	Smith	Liza	15 Tall Tree Road	4500 Greerton	F	12	2.50	N	
26	Stowerton	Laura	12 Oak St	4200 New Grove	F	12	3.00	Y	
27	Townsend	Ken	8 Waterford Dr	4000 Westport	M	15	3.00	Y	
28	Youmad	Alanna	58 Eagle St	5400 Fern Grove	F	13	2.50	Y	
29									

▷ To deactivate a list, click a cell, a row or a column outside the list; a blue border then appears around the list.

⇒ *To convert a list into a normal range of cells, open the drop-down list on the **List** button on the **List** toolbar then click the **Convert to Range** option. Click **Yes** to confirm the conversion.*

B- Using the data form

Accessing the form

▷ Click a cell in the table you are managing as a list.

▷ **Data - Form**

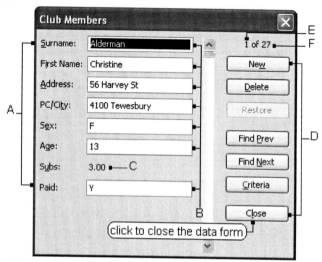

A	Field names
B	Text boxes for entering field contents
C	Contents of calculated fields
D	Command buttons
E	The number of the current record
F	The total number of records

Managing records

▷ To add a new record, click the **New** button then fill in each new record: press ⌨ to move to the next box, except after the last one; ⇧Shift ⌨ to go back to the previous box. To confirm the data entered, press Enter.

▷ To move from record to record, use the scroll bar or the arrow keys:

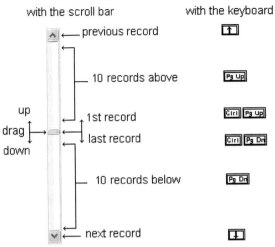

with the scroll bar   with the keyboard

- previous record
- 10 records above
- 1st record
- last record
- 10 records below
- next record

up
drag
down

▷ To delete a record, go to that record and click the **Delete** button; confirm with **OK**.
▷ To edit a record, access it, make the necessary changes then press [Enter] (the **Restore** button retrieves the former values).

⇨ *The last form displayed is always a new form, ready to be filled in.*

Finding a particular record

▷ Display either the first or last record.
▷ Click the **Criteria** button.
▷ Enter the search criteria in the same way as you would fill in a record but without pressing [Enter].

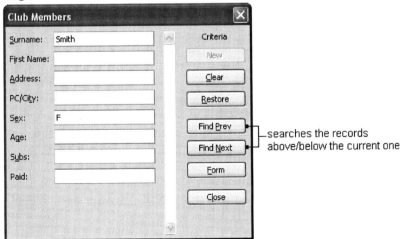

searches the records
above/below the current one

8.2 Filters

A- Creating and using a simple filter

A filter selects records that meet a set criterion.

▷ To insert drop-down AutoFilter lists on a range of cells, activate one of the cells concerned and use **Data - Filter - AutoFilter**; to insert drop-down AutoFilter lists in a list, click one of the cells in it.

Filtering by one of the values in a list

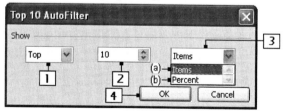

each list contains the values from the field

| 1 | [C] Open the list attached to the field in question. |
| 2 | Click the filter value. |

Excel automatically displays only the records that meet the filter value. The row numbers appear in a different colour. Excel shows the number of records filtered and the total number of records in the list on the status bar.

▷ To show all the records again, open the list on the field you have filtered and click the **(All)** option at the top of the list.

Filtering the highest and lowest values

▷ Open the field concerned and click **(Top 10...)**.

[1] Indicate whether you want top values or bottom values.

[2] Specify how many of the top/bottom values you wish to see.

<table>
<tr><td>3</td><td colspan="2">Choose:</td></tr>
<tr><td></td><td>(a)</td><td>to filter all the records corresponding to the criteria (top or bottom).</td></tr>
<tr><td></td><td>(b)</td><td>to filter a number of rows corresponding to a percentage of the total number of values in the list.</td></tr>
</table>

4 Apply the filter.

Filtering by custom criteria

▷ Click **(Custom)** in the list for the field concerned.

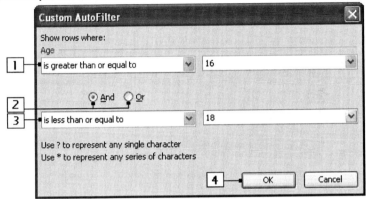

1 Give the operator and the value which make up the first filter criterion.

2 Choose **And** if both criteria must be satisfied together. Choose **Or** if either one or the other must be satisfied.

3 Enter the second condition.

4 Apply the filter.

⇨ *To combine criteria relating to several fields and connected with the "and" operator, enter the conditions in each field concerned.*

⇨ *To display all the records again, use the command **Data - Filter - Show All**.*

B - Creating and using complex filters

Creating a criteria range

▷ In a space on the worksheet, type a first row made up of the names of the fields to be used in the filter criteria. In the rows below, type the criteria:

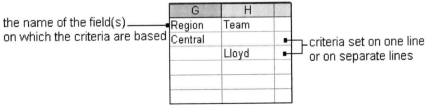

the name of the field(s) on which the criteria are based

criteria set on one line or on separate lines

▷ The criteria must be set out as follows:

OR	enter the criteria in several rows
AND	enter the criteria in several columns
AND and OR	enter the criteria in several rows and several columns

The examples below will help:

To obtain records for the Central,
West and South regions

Region
Central
West
South

To obtain records for the Central region
concerning Lloyd

Region	Team
Central	Lloyd

To obtain records for the Central region
concerning Lloyd, Allen and Carter

Region	Team
Central	Lloyd
Central	Allen
Central	Carter

⇨ *To extract MARTIN but not MARTINEZ, MARTINELLI..., enter the criteria "MARTIN" (in quotation marks).*

Using a criteria range to filter records

▷ Click inside the list and use the **Data - Filter - Advanced Filter** command.

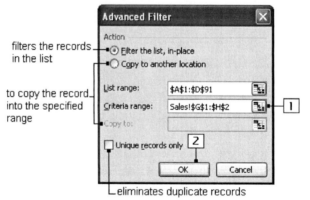

filters the records in the list

to copy the record into the specified range

eliminates duplicate records

1 Click here then select the criteria range on the worksheet.

2 Apply the filter.

⇨ *To copy the records which meet the filter criteria, the first row of the destination range (whose location is given in the **Copy to** box) must contain the names of the fields to filter.*

⇨ *If you change the criteria range, run the filter again.*

C - Calculating statistics from the records

▷ Create the appropriate criteria range then use the following functions:

=DCOUNT(database,field,criteria)	counts the cells
=DSUM(database,field,criteria)	totals the values of the field
=DAVERAGE(database,field,criteria)	calculates the average for the field
=DMAX(database,field,criteria)	extracts the maximal value in the field
=DMIN(database,field,criteria),	extracts the minimal value in the field

What the syntax refers to:

database	the reference of the cells containing the list of records (including column headings).
field	the column heading.
criteria	either the word **criteria** if you have created a complex filter or the references of the cells containing the criteria range.

⇨ *As soon as you change an item in the criteria range, Excel updates the statistics automatically.*

LISTS OF DATA

8.3 Pivot tables

A - Making a pivot table

A pivot table allows you to synthesise and analyse data from a list or an existing table.

▷ Click in the data list.

▷ **Data - PivotTable and PivotChart Report**

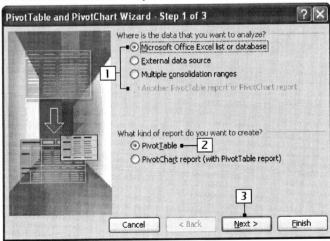

1 Indicate the data source you want to analyse.

2 If necessary, activate this option.

3 Click to continue creating the table.

▷ If necessary, select the **Range** of cells containing the data used to fill in the table then click **Next**.

▷ Click **Layout**.

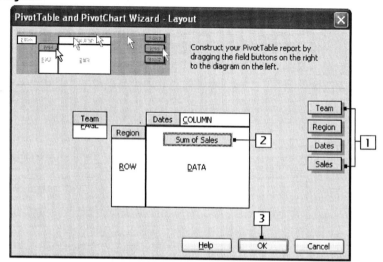

1 Drag the field labels of your choice towards the corresponding location (ROW, CO-LUMN, PAGE, DATA) to define the layout of your table.

2 Double-click a button to modify the field properties.

3 Click to continue creating the table.

▷ Indicate whether the pivot table should be created on a **New worksheet** or in an **Existing worksheet** then click **Finish**.

⇨ *If you double-click one of the result values in the data area of a pivot table, Excel displays the detail of the source data used to make that calculation in a new sheet.*

B- Modifying a pivot table

▷ To modify a pivot table, click inside the table and go through the procedure that you used to create it.

A field can also be added by dragging the corresponding field from the **PivotTable Field List** *window onto the pivot table.*

▷ To delete a field, drag the field concerned out of the pivot table.

▷ Although a pivot table is linked to the data list from which it was created, it is not updated automatically. To update the data in the pivot table, click the button on the **PivotTable** toolbar or use **Data - Refresh Data**.

▷ To change the presentation of a pivot table:

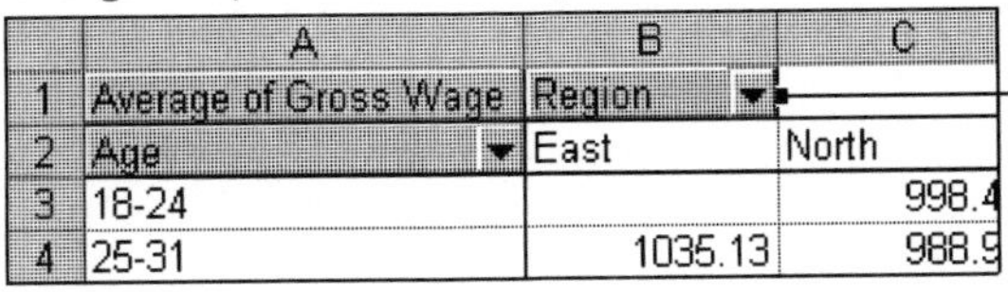

	A	B	C
1	Average of Gross Wage	Region ▼	
2	Age ▼	East	North
3	18-24		998.4
4	25-31	1035.13	988.9

click to open the list
of groups generated
by Excel and activate
or deactivate the values
you want to show or hide

▷ Format the selected cells, in the same way as you would format cells in a worksheet, or apply an automatic format (**Format - Autoformat**).

C- Grouping pivot table rows and columns

▷ Click the title of the field by which you want to group the data.

▷ **Data - Group and Outline - Group**

▷ Indicate how you want to group the data.

⇨ *To undo groups, use the* **Data - Group and Outline - Ungroup** *command.*

8.4 Pivot charts

A- Creating a pivot chart

A pivot chart is always created in conjunction with a pivot table. This means that any modifications made to the table will be automatically made to the chart, and vice versa.

▷ Access the pivot table you wish to use for the chart.

▷ Click the ▥ tool button on the **PivotTable** toolbar.

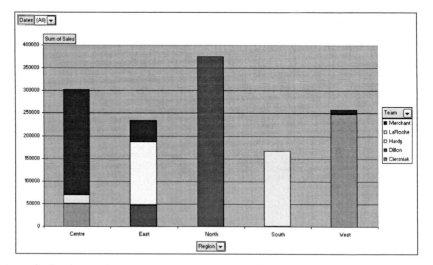

A stacked column chart appears on a separate chart sheet (stacked column is the default chart type). The row data from the pivot table become the X-axis categories and the column data become the series.

⇨ To move a pivot chart's legend, use **Chart - Chart Options - Legend** tab then choose the desired position.

⇨ It is not possible to move the labels of a pivot chart or those of its axes.

⇨ To modify the type of chart created, select the chart then use **Chart - Chart Type** and choose the desired chart type and sub-type.

⇨ To hide/show certain values, open the list attached to the field in question, then deactivate or activate the option which corresponds to the data you want to hide or show.

B- Adding/removing a field in a pivot chart

▷ Drag the field button out of the chart to remove the corresponding field. To add a field, drag it from the **PivotTable Field List** onto the chart.

If the **PivotTable Field List** window does not appear, you can display it by clicking the ▨ tool button on the **PivotTable** toolbar.

C- Moving a pivot chart

▷ Activate the chart sheet.

▷ **Chart - Location**

▷ Click the **As object in** option and give the name of the sheet to which you want to move the chart, and then click **OK**.

⇨ When you move a chart from a chart sheet, it may lose some of its formatting parameters and the chart sheet will be deleted.

9.1 Protection

A- Protecting a workbook with a password

▷ **Tools - Options - Security** tab.

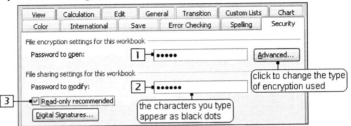

1 Enter a password to control who opens the workbook.

2 To prevent any intentional or accidental changes being saved in the workbook, enter a password here. Excel distinguishes between upper and lower case letters so take careful note of what you enter.

3 Tick this option to display a message when the workbook is opened, recommending opening it in read-only mode.

▷ Confirm, then re-enter your password(s) in the appropriate text box(es) and confirm again.

⇨ *To remove a password, use **Tools - Options - Security** tab and delete the contents of the password fields.*

⇨ *If you set opening protection, another user will not be able to open the workbook unless he/she can supply the password to open. If you set editing protection, any user not knowing the password can open the file in **Read-only** mode, but he/she will not be able to save any changes in that workbook (but they can make a copy of it).*

⇨ *You can set protection passwords as you save the workbook (**File - Save - Tools** button - **General Options**).*

B- Protecting a workbook's structure and/or windows

▷ **Tools - Protect - Protect Workbook**

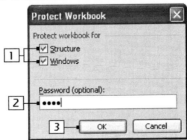

1. Select the required options:

Structure   prevents sheets from being moved, deleted, hidden, unhidden, re-named or added.

Windows   prevents the workbook window from being moved, resized, hidden or closed.

2. If you wish, set a password (up to 255 characters long) to stop any unauthorised users removing this protection.

3. Click to confirm.

▷ If you are setting a password, enter it again then click **OK**.

⇨ *To remove the protection from the workbook, use the command **Tools - Protec-tion - Unprotect Workbook**. If necessary, give the password set for protecting the sheet and click **OK**.*

C - Limiting the cells accessible to any user

1st step: unlocking selected cells

▷ Select the cells where writing is allowed.

▷ **Format - Cells** or Ctrl 1 - **Protection** tab, deactivate the **Locked** option then enter.

2nd step: protecting the sheet

▷ **Tools - Protection - Protect Sheet**

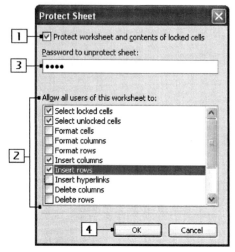

1. Make sure that this option is active.

2. Activate or deactivate the options to indicate which actions users can perform.

3. Enter a password if necessary.

4. Click to confirm.

▷ Confirm your password (if you are using one) by entering it again then click **OK**.

⇨ If you attempt to enter data in a protected cell, a warning message appears and you cannot finish your action.

⇨ Depending on the user's permissions, certain options in the **Format** menu may not be available on the protected sheet (the corresponding option names will be grey).

⇨ To remove the protection from a sheet, use the command **Tools - Protection - Unprotect Sheet**. If necessary, give the password which protects the sheet, then enter.

D - Giving certain users access to cells

When the cells in a sheet are protected, you can still grant access to certain ranges for certain users either by using different passwords or, if you are working under Windows 2000 or later, by choosing the appropriate user names.

▷ **Tools - Protection - Allow Users to Edit Ranges**

▷ Click the **New** button.

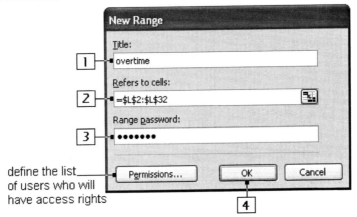

define the list of users who will have access rights

| 1 | If required, change the title for the range of cells which you are allowing access.

| 2 | Indicate the cells concerned in the worksheet.

| 3 | Enter the password that users will have to enter to be able to modify that range.

| 4 | Confirm then re-enter the password to confirm then click **OK** again.

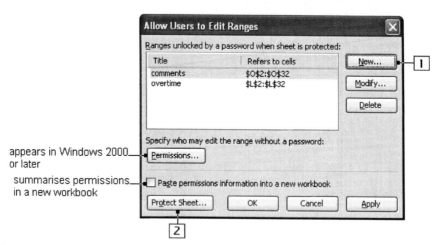

appears in Windows 2000 or later

summarises permissions in a new workbook

1. If you wish to define another range of cells controlled by a password, click the **New** button again and define further ranges.

2. Click this button, make sure the **Protect worksheet and contents of locked cells** option is active and if necessary, tick any options required in the **Allow all users of this worksheet to** list.

▷ Click **OK**.

E - Working with digital signatures

A digital signature (which is an electronic "stamp of authenticity", encrypted and secured) confirms that the file or macro comes from the signer and that nothing in it has been modified; if any changes are made to a document after signing, the signature becomes invalid. Excel manages two types of signed files: worksheets and macros. As a general rule, a file is signed to validate its contents and a macro is signed as a guarantee that it does not contain a virus.

To obtain a certificate, you can use a commercial certification authority such as VeriSign Inc., or ask your company's security administrator or other internal IT professional. You can also create a digital signature yourself (in which case, it will not be considered as authenticated). This feature requires you to install the SelfCert.exe program on your computer.

Installing the SelftCert.exe component

▷ Start by closing all open programs, then click the Windows **start** button - **Control Panel** - **Add or Remove Programs**.

▷ Click **Microsoft Office...** or **Microsoft Excel** depending on how you installed Excel and then click the **Change** button.

▷ Click **Add or Remove Features** then click **Next**.

▷ Tick the **Choose advanced customization of applications** option then click **Next**.

▷ Click the plus sign ⊞ next to **Office Shared Features** to expand the list.

▷ Click the arrow next to **Digital Signature for VBA Projects** then choose the **Run from My Computer** option.

▷ Start installation with the **Update** button.

▷ Click **OK** on the messages telling you that the installation was a success. Click the button to close the **Add or Remove Programs** dialog box.

Creating a digital certificate

▷ Click the **start** button then point to **All Programs - Microsoft Office - Microsoft Office Tools** and click **Digital Certificate for VBA Projects**.

▷ Enter **Your certificate's name** in the text box and confirm.

▷ Click **OK** on the message telling you that the new certificate was successfully created.

▷ Open the Microsoft Office Excel 2003 program again.

Signing a file

▷ Open the file you want to digitally sign.

▷ **Tools - Options - Security** tab - **Digital Signatures** button.

▷ Click the **Add** button.

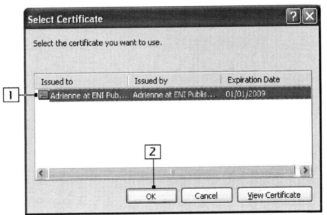

1 Select the digital certificate you want to use.

2 Click to confirm.

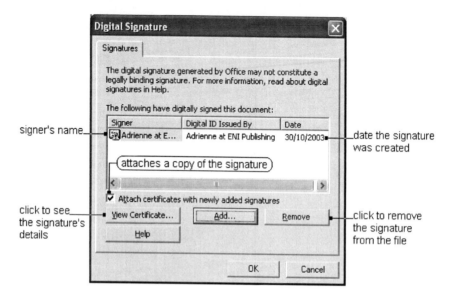

signer's name — Signer: Adrienne at E...

attaches a copy of the signature

date the signature was created

click to see the signature's details — View Certificate...

click to remove the signature from the file

▷ Click **OK** twice.

The next time you open the file, the term **[Signed, unverified]** *will appear on the title bar. If you make changes to the file and try to save them, you will see a message informing you that all the file's digital signatures will be deleted.*

Signing a macro project

▷ Open the file containing the macro project you want to sign.

▷ **Tools - Macro - Visual Basic Editor** or ⌨Alt ⌨F11

▷ In the **Project Explorer**, select the project you want to sign.

▷ **Tools - Digital Signature**

If you have not already selected a digital signature, no certificate will be suggested; otherwise the name of the last digital signature selected appears in the **Digital Signature** *window.*

▷ Click the **Choose** button to select a certificate (if the suggestion is not suitable for example); click the required certificate and click **OK** to confirm.

▷ Click **OK** in the **Digital Signature** window to digitally sign the macro project with the selected certificate.

▷ If you want to close the **Microsoft Visual Basic** window, use the **File - Close and Return to Microsoft Excel** command or ⌨Alt ⌨Q.

⇨ The **Remove** button in the **Digital Signature** dialog box deletes the signature from a macro project.

⇨ To check the macro security level, use **Tools - Options - Security** tab - **Macro Security** button. Activate the option for the security level you wish to apply and confirm.

9.2 Team work

A- Managing shared workbooks

Sharing a workbook
▷ **Tools - Share Workbook - Editing** tab
▷ Tick the **Allow changes by more than one user...** option then click **OK**.
▷ Confirm the message that offers to save the workbook.

Using a shared workbook
▷ Open the shared workbook (which will be at a network location).
The term [Shared] on the title bar indicates that you are using a shared workbook.
▷ **Tools - Options - General** tab

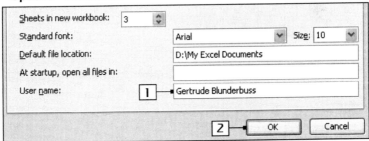

1 Enter your user name so the changes you make to the workbook are identified as yours.
2 Confirm.
▷ Enter or edit the data as you wish.

Some actions cannot be performed on shared workbooks. For example, you cannot merge cells, create charts or drawing objects, insert pictures or create subtotals or pivot tables.

▷ If required, set up your personal filter and print settings. Each user's personal settings will be saved by default.

If the original author's filter and print settings should be activated each time the workbook is opened, use Tools - Share Workbook - Advanced tab, and deactivate the Print settings and Filter settings options.

▷ Save the shared workbook with **File - Save**. This will update the file with the changes you have just made and display those that other users may have made since the last time you saved.

If the Resolve Conflicts dialog box appears, resolve the problems (cf. Resolving modification conflicts).

▷ If you want to know who currently is working on the shared workbook, use **Tools - Share Workbook - Editing** tab.

⇨ *If you would prefer other users' changes to be updated at regular intervals rather than each time the workbook is saved, go into **Tools - Share Workbook** - **Advanced** tab. In the **Update changes** frame, tick the **Automatically every** option and specify a time interval in minutes. This option can be modified independently by each user.*

Resolving modification conflicts

If you modify the same cells as another user and try to save those changes, a conflict occurs. Excel displays a dialog box that allows you to choose which changes are saved.

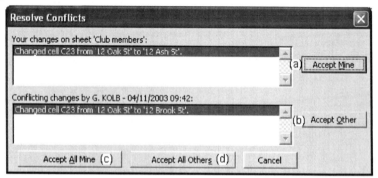

▷ To examine each conflicting change one by one, click (a) or (b) to confirm respectively your own modification or that of the other user and go on to the next modification. To accept all your changes or all those made by the other user, click (c) or (d) as required.

⇨ *If you wish to give your changes priority over those made by other users, which means that the **Resolve Conflicts** dialog box will no longer appear, activate the **The changes being saved win** option (**Tools - Share Workbook - Advanced** tab - **Conflicting changes between users** frame).*

Unsharing a workbook

▷ Make sure you are the only current user.

▷ **Tools - Share Workbook - Editing** tab

▷ Deactivate the **Allow changes by more than one user** option and click **OK**.

B- Merging workbooks

It is possible to make copies of a shared workbook, with each copy being modified by a different user independently. The copied workbooks, and their modifications, can then be merged into a single workbook.

Copying a shared workbook

▷ **Tools - Share Workbook - Editing** tab

▷ If the workbook is not yet shared, tick the **Allow changes by more than one user** option then click the **Advanced** tab.

▷ Check that the **Keep change history for** option is active in the **Track changes** frame.

If necessary, modify the number of days during which the other users can change or add comments to the copies of the shared workbook.

You will not be able to merge the copies of the workbook once this reviewing date is passed. If you are unsure about the amount of time required, enter a high number such as 1000 days.

▷ Click **OK** and if necessary, confirm saving the workbook.

▷ To make the copies of the workbook, use the **File - Save As** command and give each copy a different name.

Merging two or more workbooks

▷ Open the shared workbook in which you wish to merge the modifications made to all the copies.

▷ **Tools - Compare and Merge Workbooks**

▷ If necessary, confirm saving the workbook.

▷ In the **Select Files to Merge into Current Workbook** dialog box, select the copy or copies of the shared workbook whose changes you wish to merge.

To select several files, use ⇧ Shift *to select adjacent files or* Ctrl *to select nonadjacent ones.*

▷ Click **OK** to start the merge.

C - Tracking changes

Tracking the changes in a shared workbook

▷ Open the shared workbook then use **Tools - Track Changes - Highlight Changes**.

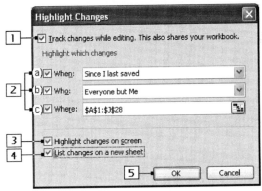

1 Activate this option.

2 Indicate the changes that you want to see highlighted:

    (a)   Choose the time interval that interests you.

    (b)   Choose the users whose changes should be highlighted.

    (c)   Choose to highlight the changes in a specific range of cells.

If none of the three options are active, Excel will pick out all the changes made by all the users of the shared workbook, including your own.

$\boxed{3}$ Tick this check box if you want Excel to mark the changes directly in the cells.

$\boxed{4}$ Choose this option to show all the changes as a list in a new sheet called **History**. This list can be filtered.

$\boxed{5}$ Click to confirm.

Accepting or rejecting changes in a shared workbook

▷ Open the shared workbook then use **Tools - Track Changes - Accept or Reject Changes**.

▷ If Excel offers to save the workbook, click **OK**.

indicate the type of changes you want to review

If none of these three options are active, Excel reviews all the changes made to the shared workbook.

▷ Click **OK**.

*The modification details appear in the **Accept or Reject Changes** dialog box and the first modification is highlighted in the workbook.*

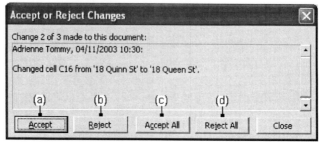

▷ Choose (a) or (b) to check each change; Excel will then go on to the next change automatically. If several changes have been made in the same cell, Excel will ask you to choose one of the values; if this occurs, click the required value then click (a); you can use the (c) or (d) button to process all the changes in a single action.

D-Protecting a shared workbook

You should activate this protection before sharing the workbook.

▷ Open the workbook that is not currently shared then use **Tools - Protection - Protect and Share Workbook**.

▷ Tick the **Sharing with track changes** option.

▷ To prevent other users from removing the protection, enter a **Password**.

▷ Click **OK** then enter the password again to confirm it and click **OK** again.

▷ Confirm saving the workbook.

*The workbook is shared automatically. The **Allow changes by more than one user** options under the **Editing** tab and the **Track changes** option under the **Advanced** tab (**Tools - Share Workbook**) are no longer available.*

⇨ *To remove the protection, and stop the workbook from being shared, use the **Tools - Protection - Unprotect Shared Workbook** command, enter the password if necessary and confirm.*

E- Sending a workbook for review

If you want one or more colleagues to review a workbook, you can send them a link to the workbook saved on a network or send them a copy of it. This command can be used only if you have Outlook 2002 or later.

▷ Open the workbook you wish to send for review then use **File - Send To - Mail Recipient (for Review)**.

▷ If the workbook you wish to send is saved on your hard disk, Excel may prompt you to saved a shared version of the workbook. If you want to track changes or merge changes at a later time, click **Yes** and indicate where to save the copy, otherwise click **No**.

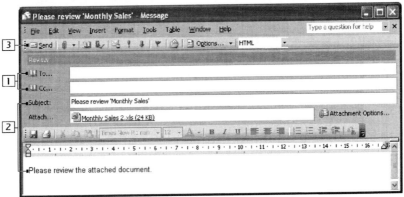

1 Give the address(es) to which you are sending the workbook and also any to which you are sending a copy.

2 If necessary, change the message subject and enter any further comments in the main message pane.

3 Click to send the message.

⇨ *The recipient receives a message containing (depending on the options chosen as you prepared it) an attached workbook file and/or a link to the file on a network. The recipient can make changes to the workbook and return it to the sender by using the **File - Send To - Original Sender** command. This message can be modified in the usual ways and sent using the **Send** button.*

10.1 Toolbars

A- Creating a toolbar

▷ **View - Toolbars - Customize - Toolbars** tab
▷ Click the **New** button.
▷ Enter a name for the toolbar and confirm.
  A tiny floating toolbar appears on the screen.
▷ To add tools to the bar, activate the **Commands** tab and drag the required options from the **Customize** dialog box towards the new bar.
▷ When you have added all the buttons to the bar, click the **Close** button on the **Customize** dialog box.

B- Managing tools on an open toolbar

Deleting a tool button

▷ **View - Toolbars - Customize**
▷ Drag the tool button you wish to delete off the displayed toolbar away from any other toolbar or menu and close the dialog box.

Adding a tool button or menu

▷ **View - Toolbars - Customize**
▷ Activate the **Commands** tab.

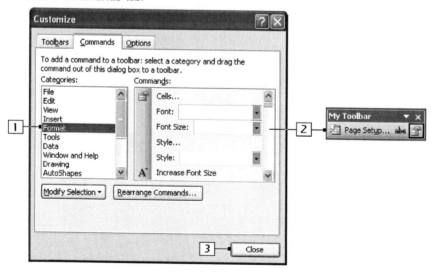

1 Select the category containing the tool you want to add, or the **Built-in Menus** category to add a menu.
2 Drag the tool button or the menu from the dialog box onto a toolbar or menu bar.

Excel 2003

| 3 | Close the dialog box.

⇨ Once you have modified a toolbar, you can retrieve the original bar by clicking the **Reset** button in the **Customize** dialog box, **Toolbars** tab.

⇨ At the far right of some toolbars, you can click the 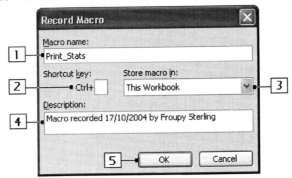 symbol to add or remove certain buttons.

⇨ To move a tool button on a toolbar when the **Customize** dialog box is closed, hold down the ⌐Alt⌐ key and drag the tool button to the required position.

0.2 Macros

A- Creating/deleting a macro

▷ If necessary, open the workbook concerned by the macro.

▷ **Tools - Macros - Record New Macro**

| 1 | Give the macro a name.

| 2 | If you wish, specify a shortcut key which will run the macro.

| 3 | Indicate where the macro is to be stored: if you want the macro to be permanently accessible, choose **Personal Macro Workbook** (this workbook is opened then hidden, each time you start Excel).

| 4 | If necessary, change the macro description.

| 5 | Click to create the macro.

▷ Go through all the actions to be automated in the macro.

▷ When all the actions have been recorded, click the ⌐■⌐ button on the **Stop Rec.** bar.

⇨ To delete a macro, use **Tools - Macro - Macros**, select the macro concerned then click **Delete** followed by **Yes** to confirm the deletion.

B- Running a macro

▷ If a macro has been created in a workbook other than PERSONAL.XLS, open the workbook.

▷ **Tools - Macro - Macros** or [Alt][F8]

▷ Double-click the macro you want to run.

⇨ *You can also run it by pressing the shortcut key defined when the macro was created.*

C- Loading an Add-In

These tools are provided with Excel but are not automatically loaded.

▷ **Tools - Add-Ins**

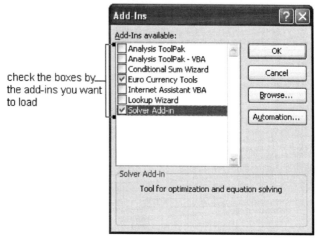

check the boxes by the add-ins you want to load

⇨ *Add-ins appear as options in different Excel menus.*

D- Viewing the contents of a macro

▷ If the macro is stored in PERSONAL.XLS, use the command **Window - Unhide** to display it, as you would for any other hidden workbook.

▷ **Tools - Macro - Macros** or [Alt][F8]

▷ Select the macro, then click **Edit**.

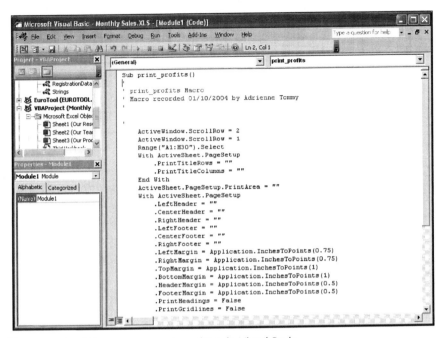

The contents of the macro appear, written in Visual Basic.

10.3 Web pages

A- Creating a hyperlink to a file/web page

▷ Select the cell in which you want to create the link.

▷ **Insert**
  Hyperlink

Ctrl K

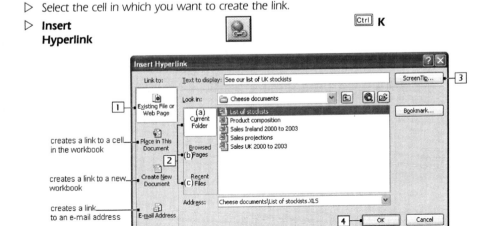

creates a link to a cell in the workbook

creates a link to a new workbook

creates a link to an e-mail address

1 If necessary, select this option.

2 Depending on the type of document the link must point to, click a button to select:

(a)   a target file for the link within the current folder,

(b)   a target web page in the list of browsed pages,

(c)   a target file for the list in the list of recently used files,

or enter the exact file path of the document towards which you are making the link, if you know it.

3 If necessary, enter the text that should appear in a ScreenTip when you point to the link. Confirm with **OK**.

4 Finish creating the hyperlink.

	A	B	C	D	E
1	**Dutch cheese**				
2					
3		1st Qtr	2nd Qtr	3rd Qtr	
4	Edam	12456	13580	14200	
5	Gouda	18744	11456	13088	
6	Maasdam	12369	9632	10703	
7	Leyden	9630	7112	8336	
8					
9	See our list of UK stockists				
10					
11	Click this link to see the list of stores selling our finest farmhouse cheeses.				
12					
13	click the link to open its target document				
14					

⇨ To remove a hyperlink, click the link, holding down the mouse button a few seconds, to select the cell (a simple click will activate the link), then press the [Del] key.

⇨ If you do not want e-mail addresses to automatically appear in the form of hyperlinks, use **Tools - AutoCorrect Options - AutoFormat As You Type** tab and deactivate the **Internet and network paths with hyperlinks** check box.

B - Creating and/or publishing a web page

You can publish a web page with or without interactivity.

To work in an interactive web page (one which is modifiable), users of the page must have Internet Explorer 4.01 or later installed, as well as a Microsoft Office licence for using worksheets, charts and pivot table lists published exclusively from Microsoft Excel.

▷ Create or open the workbook containing the data you want to publish.

▷ If you want to publish only one of the sheets in the workbook, activate it by clicking its tab.

▷ **File - Save as Web Page**

▷ Select where you want to save the web page using the **Save In** list and/or the places bar. There is a button on the places bar that leads to **My Network Places**.

▷ In the dialog box, use the **Web Options** in the **Tools** menu to change the publication settings (target browser, managing published files, encoding, fonts etc.).

▷ Activate the **Selection** or **Entire Workbook** option.

Only individual worksheets can be published with interactivity.

▷ Tick **Add interactivity** if necessary.

▷ If you wish, click the **Change Title** button to enter the text that will be displayed in the browser's title bar when the web page is opened, then click **OK**.

▷ If necessary, edit the suggested **File name**.

▷ To save the web page, without setting any publication options, click **Save**.

The web page appears in html format and the original file closes automatically (if you create an interactive file, Excel does not generate any supporting files folder).

▷ To publish the web page on a server, click the **Publish** button.

A new dialog box opens:

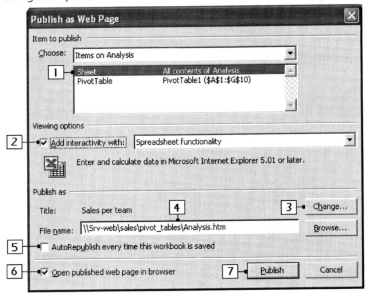

☐1 Select the item you wish to publish (this list varies according to the web page's contents).

☐2 If necessary, tick this option then open the attached list to select the Excel functionality that you want to make available to users of the page.

☐3 If necessary, change the title entered during the previous stage.

☐4 If necessary, modify the address where the page will be published.

☐5 Tick this option if you want the web page to be updated each time you save changes to its source file.

☐6 Tick this option to see the finished web page in a browser as soon as you finish publishing it.

VARIOUS ADVANCED FEATURES

7 Confirm publishing the page.

*If you publish a pivot table, your browser may tell you that the source data are stored on another domain. If this occurs, click **Yes** to continue.*

Excel publishes the web page in htm format, plus any supporting files folder that may exist, in the chosen location (hard disk or web server); the original file in xls format remains in its initial location on your hard disk.

⇨ *To see a workbook as it would look on the Internet or an intranet, use **File - Web Page Preview**; the default browser opens and shows the workbook as a web page.*

⇨ *To delete a web page, use the Windows Explorer to go to the folder and/or server where the file is stored, select the web page (file_name.htm) and if necessary its supporting files folder (file_name_files) and press the* Del *key.*

Working with menus and options

Display shortcut menu   `⇧ Shift` `F10`

File

New	`Ctrl` N	Save As	`F12`
Open	`Ctrl` O	Print	`Ctrl` P
Save	`Ctrl` S	Exit	`Alt` `F4`

Edit

Undo	`Ctrl` Z	Clear	
Repeat	`Ctrl` Y	Contents	`Del`
Cut	`Ctrl` X	Delete	`Ctrl` -
Copy	`Ctrl` C	Find	`Ctrl` F
Paste	`Ctrl` V	Next	`⇧ Shift` `F4`
Fill		Previous	`Ctrl` `⇧ Shift` `F4`
Down	`Ctrl` D	Replace	`Ctrl` H
Right	`Ctrl` R	Go To	`F5` or `Ctrl` G

Insert

Cells, Rows, Columns	`Ctrl` +	Name	
Worksheet	`⇧ Shift` `F11`	Define	`Ctrl` `F3`
Chart		Paste	`F3`
As New Sheet	`F11`	Create	`Ctrl` `⇧ Shift` `F3`
Cell comment	`⇧ Shift` `F2`	Hyperlink	`Ctrl` K

Format

Cells, Object etc.	`Ctrl` 1	Column	
Row		Hide	`Ctrl` 0 (alphanumeric keyboard)
Hide	`Ctrl` 9 ((alphanumeric keyboard)	Unhide	`Ctrl` `⇧ Shift` 0
Unhide	`Ctrl` `⇧ Shift` 9	Style	`Alt` '

Tools

Spelling	`F7`	Calculation	
Research	`Alt`-click	Calculate Now	`F9`
Formula Auditing		Calculate Worksheet	`⇧ Shift` `F9`
Mode	`Ctrl` `		
Macro			
Macros	`Alt` `F8`		
Visual Basic Editor	`Alt` `F11`		
Microsoft Script Editor	`Alt` `⇧ Shift` `F4`		

Data

Group and Outline	
Group	`Alt` `⇧ Shift` `→`
Ungroup	`Alt` `⇧ Shift` `←`
List	
Create List	`Ctrl` L

Help

Microsoft Excel Help	`F1`

Other key combinations

Entering data

Enter the current date   `Ctrl` `;`
Enter the current time   `Ctrl` `⇧ Shift` `:`
Euro symbol   `Alt Gr` **4**
Insert same formula/
value as cell above   `Ctrl` `'`
Insert value only
from cell above   `Ctrl` `⇧ Shift` **"**

Insert Autosum   `Alt` **=**
Clear selection
of formulas/data   `Del`
Tab within a text box   `Ctrl` `⇄`
Display list of
AutoComplete entries   `Alt` `↓`

Working in the Formula Bar

Activate Edit mode in cell
and formula bar   `F2`
Start a formula   **=**
Delete from insertion point
to the end of line   `Ctrl` `Del`
Insert a line break   `Alt` `Enter`
Cancel unconfirmed entry   `Esc`
Confirm cell entry   `Enter`
Fill selected range
with the current entry   `Ctrl` `Enter`

Confirm an array formula   `Ctrl` `⇧ Shift` `Enter`
Create relative/
absolute references   `F4`
After a function has been
entered, displays the
formula palette   `Ctrl` **A**
After a function has been
entered, displays function
arguments   `Ctrl` `⇧ Shift` **A**

Formatting cells

Apply an outline border   `Ctrl` `⇧ Shift` **&**
Remove all borders   `Ctrl` `⇧ Shift` **-**
Apply or remove bold type   `Ctrl` **B**

Apply or remove italic type   `Ctrl` **I**
Apply or remove
an underline   `Ctrl` **U**

Formatting numbers and dates

Apply General format   `Ctrl` `⇧ Shift` **~**
Thousands, two decimal
places plus separator   `Ctrl` `⇧ Shift` **!**
Currency format, two
decimal places   `Ctrl` `⇧ Shift` **$**

Exponential number format,
two decimal places   `Ctrl` `⇧ Shift` **^**
Date format, dd-mmm-yy
(01-Jan-01)   `Ctrl` **#**

Moving in worksheets

Beginning of current row
A1 on current sheet   `Ctrl`
Cell at intersection
of column used furthest
to the right and row used
furthest down   `Ctrl` `End`
Next window   or

Previous window    or

Next sheet in the
workbook   `Ctrl` `Pg Dn`
Previous sheet
in the workbook   `Ctrl` `Pg Up`
Next pane
in a split worksheet   `F6`
Previous pane
in a split worksheet   `⇧ Shift` `F6`

Excel 2003

Selecting

Whole sheet	`Ctrl` A
Whole column	`Ctrl` `space`
Whole row	`⇧ Shift` `space`

Activates/deactivates extend mode	`F8`
Add a range of cells to current selection	`⇧ Shift` `F8`

Selecting of individual cells

Cells containing comments	`Ctrl` `⇧ Shift` O
Rectangular range of cells surrounding the active cell	`Ctrl` `⇧ Shift` *
The entire array to which the cell belongs	`Ctrl` /
Only cells to which the formulas in the selection make direct reference	`Ctrl` [
All cells to which formulas in the selection make direct or indirect reference	`Ctrl` `⇧ Shift` [
Only cells with formulas that refer directly to the active cell	`Ctrl`]
All cells with formulas that refer directly or indirectly to the active cell	`Ctrl` `⇧ Shift`]
Only visible cells in the current selection	`Alt` ;
Select cells in a selected row whose contents are different from the active cell	`Ctrl` \
Select cells in a selected column whose contents are different from the comparison cell in each column; for each column the comparison cell is on the same row as the active cell	`Ctrl` `⇧ Shift` \

Outlines

Group rows or columns	`Alt` `⇧ Shift` `→`
Ungroup rows or columns	`Alt` `⇧ Shift` `←`
Display/hide outline symbols	`Ctrl` 8

A

ADD-IN

B

BORDER

C

CALCULATIONS

CATEGORY

CELLS

See also EDITING DATA, ENTERING DATA,
ROWS/COLUMNS

CHARACTER

CHART

See also DATA SERIES,
PIVOT CHART

COMMENT

CONDITION

Excel 2003

D

E

INDEX

F

L

M

N

O

P

R

RECORD

RESEARCH

REVIEWING

ROWS/COLUMNS

S

SCALING

SCENARIO

SELECTING

SHARING

SORTING

SOUND

SPELLING

STATISTICS

STYLES

SYMBOLS

T

TABS

TASK PANE

TEMPLATE

TIME

TITLES

TOOL BUTTON

TOOLBARS

TOOLS

V

VIDEO

VIEWS

Excel 2003

W

WEB PAGE
Creating/publishing   108
Previewing   110

WORDART
Inserting in a sheet   80

WORKBOOK
Closing   13
Copying/moving a sheet from one workbook
to another   17
Creating   14
Displaying/hiding   8
Managing shared workbooks   99
Opening   12
Previewing as web page   110
Protecting   93
Protecting structure and/or windows   93
Saving   12
Sending for review   103
Signing digitally   97

See also TEMPLATE

WORKGROUP
Linking several worksheets   17

WORKSHEET
Applying a modification to several worksheets   17
Changing the colour of worksheet tabs   18
Consolidating   41
Copying cells into several sheets   27
Copying/moving from one workbook
to another   17
Deleting   18
Displaying/hiding   8
Inserting   18
Limiting access to cells   94
Moving from one sheet to another   10
Naming   18
Printing   61
Selecting to create a workgroup   17
Splitting   6

Z

ZOOMING
In the workspace   7

INDEX